ONEWORLD PUBLICATIONS

THE UNIVERSE WITHIN

Dr Anjam Khursheed is a senior lecturer at the National University of Singapore. He obtained his doctorate from Edinburgh University, and he has written a number of scientific papers in the area of computational electron optics and electromagnetic fields, as well as books on religious and philosophical issues.

By the same author:

Science and Religion: Towards the Restoration of an Ancient Harmony

ANJAM KHURSHEED

The UNIVERSE Within

An Exploration of the Human Spirit

ONEWORLD
OXFORD

THE UNIVERSE WITHIN

Oneworld Publications
(Sales and Editorial)
185 Banbury Road
Oxford OX2 7AR
England

Oneworld Publications
(U.S. Marketing Office)
42 Broadway
Rockport, MA 01966
USA

ISBN 1-85168-075-6

Printed and bound by
WSOY, Finland

Contents

Acknowledgements

I gratefully acknowledge the help of Jan Nikolic, whose careful editing and thought-provoking questions greatly improved the original manuscript. Thanks must also go to Bill Hynd, who read an early version of the manuscript and provided much-appreciated positive feedback. I am in debt also to Khazeh Fananapazir for providing me with some reference material. Lastly, I would like to acknowledge the support of my wife Antonella, who gave me the necessary time and encouragement to make several revisions of the manuscript.

Introduction: The Broken Image

Are we the central actors in a cosmic drama? Is this planet earth a heavenly home, or a temporary hovel en route to paradise, or merely another gravestone in an eternal cemetery? Are we, as the Bible tells us, 'a little lower than the angels', 'crowned with glory and honour' – made in 'God's image'? Or are we merely walking bags of chemical compounds moulded in the image of chromosomes – puppets pulled along by selfish genes? Why are we the only animal for whom existence seems to pose an insoluble riddle? Why are we the only animal to whom life seems tragic? Are we worth more than the dust beneath our feet? As Shakespeare's Hamlet puts it:

> What a piece of work is a man! how noble in reason! how infinite in faculty! in form and moving how express and admirable! in action how like an angel! in apprehension how like a god! the beauty of the world! the paragon of animals! And yet, to me, what is this quintessence of dust?[1]

Humanity stands on the dividing line between two universes: the conscious universe within us and the external universe that surrounds us. All human beings have been faced with the challenge of knowing themselves, and knowing the world around them. Our history unfolds as a drama of countless selves, of conscious human beings with their sufferings, their joys, their sacrifices, their aspirations, their despairs, their loves, their hates, grappling to find their own unique place in a universe that both contains them, and extends far beyond them. When pondering our position in the greater cosmos, who is not engulfed by a feeling of being infinitely small? In the cosmological scale of things, who is not seized by a profound sense of isolation? Do we not appear to be tiny pieces of stellar dust momentarily coalesced together on the surface of an insignificant planet, located within an unimportant solar system, in a remote corner of a galaxy, swallowed up by vast regions of space, dwarfed by a universe stretching out to infinity? Our place in the universe is so minuscule that it defies all our attempts at conceptualizing it.

And yet, we have an existence, and to our loved ones and our close friends it is an important existence. For them, we do not need to justify it, because in their human cosmologies we are as galaxies. Like all human beings we are conscious, we have our own identities, our own memories, our own hopes and ideals. Human beings have their intelligence, their art, their science, and their civilizations. And all this is not insignificant. Each human being is a galaxy of thoughts, feelings and talents, and each society is a cosmos of such galaxies.

This tension between the individuality of human lives and the vastness of the cosmos surely underlies the most fundamental dynamics of our being. The philosopher Immanuel Kant put it this way: 'Two things fill the mind with ever new and increasing admiration and awe, the oftener and more steadily we reflect upon them: the starry heavens above me and the moral law within me.'[2]

From the moment of birth to the instant of death a human being is struggling to strike a balance between the conscious world within and the world outside. At birth children are unable to differentiate themselves from the external world, and as they progress through infancy, childhood and adolescence their consciousness and will seem to grow steadily stronger. Consciousness of ourselves dawns upon us. And like the sun gradually rising in the morning, the light of consciousness and self-knowledge shines steadily stronger as our lives progress. Then, like the sun setting in western skies, consciousness slips away. For a brief time, consciousness seems to fix onto our bodies and light up our eyes, and then, without any explanation, is withdrawn. During that brief time between its coming and going, we wonder who we are, where we came from, where we are, and where we are going. We gaze out onto a universe twinkling with starlight, seen in the momentary flicker of our own inner light. An inner flame lights up within our bodies, experiences joy, pain, sorrow, love, searches for meaning, and then disappears. None of this comes with a ready explanation; all is mystery.

Our existence involves a constant conflict between the impersonal and the personal; it is a struggle to make our own unique mark on a world apparently indifferent to our conscious presence. At each stage of life, a human being must establish a place for his or her desires, hopes and fears – to obtain recognition of the autonomy and self-identity of his or her mind. Human life often seems to be a battleground between mind and matter, and if we are fortunate enough to live through these conflicts, the wounds and scars we bear appear to help our minds grow stronger and wiser.

A similar process seems to be occurring in humanity's collective life on earth. At the beginning of human evolution on this planet, primitive human beings were prisoners of nature; their world was dominated almost entirely by events external to their minds. Yet consciousness gradually dawned upon our species – exactly how and why, nobody knows. Ever since this beginning, human consciousness seems to have grown steadily stronger. Primitive human beings explained the world outside in terms of the world within themselves, projecting their inner lives onto their outer lives. Their vision was primarily anthropocentric. Each society developed its own method of establishing a harmony between mind and matter, some seeming to deny the separate existence of matter altogether, while others diminished the importance of mind.

From our distant origins through to modern societies, our collective will and consciousness seem to have been growing progressively stronger, so that it now appears that events in nature are dependent on humanity or, more accurately, on the human mind. Yet modern men and women claim their vision of the world is the reverse of the primitive one; the modern vision is not anthropocentric, but objective. We do not see the world around us in terms of our inner world, but rather see everything, including ourselves, in terms of the external universe. The modern mind, although in practice master of earthly matter, in popular theory denies itself any cosmic significance and claims only to be a prisoner of the world of nature – to be moulded out of natural forces.

Although this view, which can be called the scientific world view, has dramatically enhanced our knowledge of the universe around us, it is questionable how much it has revealed about the conscious universe within us. During this century alone, our impact upon the external world has been unparalleled in human history. We have conquered our immediate cosmic neighbour – by landing on its surface. We have pushed back frontiers that previously imprisoned us, and our external vision seems limitless. The spirit behind these conquests of the external world seems to be indomitable, and no natural barriers seem capable of containing the modern human mind. From the infinitely small to the cosmologically large, the human mind can contemplate vistas of new worlds; it can anticipate the course of events in the world of nature, from the atom to the star. The distances that used to separate members of the human race have shrunk dramatically, and the external universe does not seem so threatening since astronomical knowledge has penetrated through vast expanses of space and time, perhaps even, it is said, to the beginning of the universe itself.

Yet many believe that in contrast to the impressive gains in our knowledge of the external world, our knowledge of ourselves remains limited. Some would go even further and suggest that the modern picture of human nature is a hopelessly fragmented one. The modern person's view of himself has been likened to a 'broken image', where the traditional picture of humanity made in God's image has been irreversibly shattered.[3] The philosopher and mathematician Alfred Whitehead has described the 'bifurcation of nature' as a fundamental component in modern thought: our human experience has been divided into two separate realms, the quantitative world of science and the qualitative world of human emotions and values.[4] This divide has also been referred to as a 'clash between two cultures', a conflict between the scientific and the humanistic (the artistic, the religious and so on) in our society.[5]

In modern societies, the scientific approach is the publicly accepted one, while our moral lives are relegated to a limbo world of private convictions. This tragic split in our consciousness has been described as our 'modern dilemma', one that divides our minds from our hearts.[6] It is as if over the past few hundred years, our consciousness has been gradually withdrawn from nature. Some have suggested that the process began from the very inception of the modern scientific outlook, and has now left our consciousness precariously perched on our lives like a 'ghost in a machine'.[7]

The modern scientific world-view can suggest that we are no more than mere fragments of matter in a world that appears to be neither about us nor for us. The philosopher Bertrand Russell, writing around the time of World War I, described this as follows:

> Such, in outline, but even more purposeless, more void of meaning, is the world which Science presents for our belief. Amid such a world, if anywhere, our ideals hence forward must find a home. That man is a product of causes which had no provision of the end they were achieving; that his origin, his growth, his hopes and fears, his loves and his beliefs, are but the outcome of accidental collocations of atoms; that no fire, no heroism, no intensity of thought and feeling, can preserve an individual life beyond the grave; that all the labours of the ages, all the devotion, all the inspirations, all the noonday brightness of human genius, are destined to extinction in the vast death of the solar system, and the whole temple of Man's achievement must inevitably be buried beneath the debris of a universe in ruins – all these things, if not quite beyond dispute, are yet so nearly certain, that no philosophy which rejects them can hope to stand.[8]

Thus, human lives are denied any special significance in the cosmos on the basis of a picture provided by modern science. The authority of science is invoked to argue that we and our status in the universe are 'void of meaning'. Traditional religious doctrines about human nature allowed for some measure of human purpose in the cosmos, but this 'modern' view of human nature is profoundly impersonal.

Much has been written about alienation in our society. Whether it be on the basis of race, sex, religion, class, creed or culture, the rebellion against perceived suppression of human identities and ideals has been a major theme of modern serious literature. Little, however, has been written on perhaps the most profound of all forms of alienation, the haunting modern sense of alienation from the cosmos. The rejection of human intuitions of purpose and identity at the universal level is often linked to the findings of modern science, and has been extremely influential in recent times. But is it really fair to attribute such a cosmologically impersonal view of humanity to modern science? This is the question that will be examined in the following pages.

In contrast to the insignificance of human life implied by this view, our inner feelings tell us that all human lives are unquestionably precious, unique and irreplaceable. In the words of the philosopher Karl Popper, 'they are selves; they are ends in themselves'.[9] Every time a person dies, a whole universe disappears with him or her. The modern impersonal approach denies the importance of human beings, while our own experience raises it to an immeasurable degree. This is our 'modern dilemma': science has been used to argue that human beings are merely objects among other objects, while our human experience tells us that we are something infinitely more valuable – human beings who live in a world of spiritual intentions, desires, hopes and meanings.

Critics of the modern impersonal world-view have linked it to the many forms of social alienation and manipulation that pervade contemporary western culture. It has been accused of creating a climate whereby people are regarded as no more than subjects for experimentation, control and manipulation; where nature is looked upon as an inanimate object ripe for exploitation.[10, 11, 12] In the words of one critic, this dehumanizing approach is like looking at the world with the 'eyes of a dead man',[13] dead to the warmth of our human relationships, dead to our ideals, passions, humour, hopes and purposes. It is important to recognize that this criticism of modern science does not simply refer to the harmful effects of technology – alarming and important though these are. It is not simply that machines have made human contact more remote, or that methods of mass production have numbed our appreciation of arts and crafts, or that industrial wastelands have come between us and nature. All these effects are merely the symptoms of an inner sickness that cannot be adequately identified in the external world – it is rooted in our minds, and hence all the more difficult to cure. The modern divide is not simply the gap between scientist and artist, or between scientist and clergyman, although these undoubtedly exist. It is something much more fundamental and subtle; in its most profound sense, it is a mental divide. Our actions, our thoughts, our experiences, our relationships, our hopes, our perceptions of our place in the cosmos, all reflect a shattered self-image. Our inner vision is split, and the shadows of its fragments are cast upon all that we see.

The 'modern dilemma' is a schism caused by human self-alienation.[14] Not only are human beings in danger of becoming servants to technology, but critics of the modern world-view fear the human spirit has been crushed by the vast impersonal machine of science.[15] Some writers on modern society claim science is inherently dehumanizing – dead to our humanity.[16] 'Man', in the words of one writer, 'resists objectification; and if his resistance to it is broken, man himself is broken'.[17] But is it really science that causes the fragmentation of the human spirit?

Pre-modern human beings viewed themselves and nature in a way that can broadly be termed as spiritual. Their explanation of the conscious world inside themselves and the physical world outside stemmed from their perception of a higher world, the divine world. Pre-modern human beings linked their inner and outer universes by pointing to the divine connection between them. The two worlds found unity in the world of God. An influential strand in modern thinking denies such a transcendental point of reference, and nothing has as yet replaced this link between our minds and hearts.

There is another dimension to our moral confusion. Today, humankind is faced with unprecedented challenges. The many scientific advances of the past 300 years or so have brought before us problems of such magnitude and complexity that they threaten our very existence on this planet. Indeed, the survival of all forms of life on earth is dependent on humanity exchanging its present policy of exploiting nature for one of being in harmony with nature. The ecology of the earth is in the process of suffering irreversible damage.

Few would deny that our immense global problems call for a decisive, united and courageous response on the part of ordinary people and governments everywhere if untold suffering and loss are to be averted. It is a time that calls for great spiritual resolve, a time to draw deeply on the best human ideals and aspirations. It is no longer possible to believe that the solution to the world's problems lies solely in yet undiscovered advances in science and technology, a view that prevailed until only a few decades ago. More and more people are becoming aware of the need to change our attitudes, to transform our values. Many of our problems are created by obsolescent modes of thinking. The ecological crisis is now recognized to be a crisis not about our environment but about ourselves.

Yet in the hour of what may be our greatest spiritual and moral challenge, the human race is half-hearted about moral matters and looks upon the spiritual with a certain detached scepticism. This is not a time for moral hesitation, yet there is much at the root of our thinking that casts doubt on the very foundation of morality. It is a difficult task to transform our values collectively and decisively when moral convictions are regarded as inherently private, when human values are considered to be arbitrary, and when our minds are regarded as nothing but 'ghosts in a machine'.

Where in a society dominated by impersonal facts is there a place for human values? Where do human values reside in a world governed by blind particle interactions? How can we act with decision and in unity when we are afflicted by a crisis of values? This is inextricably linked to our crisis of self-identity: when we have no coherent self-image, how can we be sure about what we value? How can one freely and courageously transform outmoded values when human beings are regarded as puppets pulled along by selfish genes? The characteristic feature of our age is that a singularly rapid expansion of scientific and technological power is accompanied by an equally momentous fragmentation of spiritual values.

Nor can this crisis of the human spirit be described as confined to the economically developed nations. The rapid implantation of western technological culture in virtually every part of the world entails an assimilation of the spiritually fragmented values underlying it. Along with the acquisition of an unceasing flow of material goods, therefore, the poorer nations are importing our moral confusion and doubt. While the West is reaping the rewards of creating an ever wider circle of economic markets to serve its hungry technological machine, it is also eroding the world's traditional value systems. Technological progress is sold with a promise of material wealth, but this has seemed inevitably to involve adopting an ideology of rampant materialism and unbridled individualism. Indeed, the fact that technological progress necessarily opposes traditional forms of wisdom is the unwritten condition under which material goods are sold around the globe. It is a transaction that day by day reveals its inherent contradictions.[18] But the entire world has invested its future in a modern world-view, and its successes or failures, its philosophical problems and cultural fragmentations, affect us all.

We are very close to an end of a millennium. The timing is apt; here is an opportunity for us to ponder our position within the context of past millennia. Our modern problems of catastrophic environmental damage, the dangers of biological, chemical or nuclear warfare, of overpopulation, international terrorism, genetic engineering and so on are quite different from the problems faced by societies living a thousand years ago. Or are they? Perhaps the medieval drama is still playing itself out, and it is only our costumes and props that have changed.

This book explores the relationship between the two worlds of our existence. In particular, it asks whether the rupture that has occurred between our inner and outer worlds can ever be mended, or whether one could even reasonably expect this chasm to be bridged. The approach taken is a philosophical one, having recourse to elements from the philosophies of science, mind, religion and so on. Because of the magnitude of the subject, the discussion will be a multi-disciplinary one. The basic premiss of the book is that one does not have to be a specialist in any branch of science, philosophy or theology to seek answers to the ultimate questions of our existence. The questions are so fundamental that all of us should ask them and all attempts at answering them must

teach us something. It is in this spirit that I undertook the writing
of this book.

In Part 1, the psychological impact of the modern impersonal
world-view on traditional western culture is examined. This
section discusses the reorientation in our thinking about
humanity's position in the cosmos and the change in our
existential self-esteem. It is argued that certain strands of modern
thought, such as a secular form of empiricism, or positivist science,
have unnecessarily widened the psychological divide between
humanity and the cosmos. When such speculative philosophies are
translated into rigid methodologies and applied to the exclusion of
all else, they are self-defeating, and ultimately lead to a fragmented
human self-image. Part 1 also describes the clash of various
conflicting images of human nature, which is characteristic of
modern thought.

In Part 2, the foundations of science are shown to be
inherently spiritual in character. Science relies on creative
qualities of the mind, as opposed to any methodology based upon
empirical observations and logical rules. Examples are taken from
the history of modern science to demonstrate that it is primarily
founded on personal knowledge and community values. The
discussion shows that modern science cannot be used to deny
humanity a place in the cosmos.

In Part 3, the psychology of the modern impersonal world-view
is examined. It is demonstrated that both science and religion can
be approached in impersonal terms, and examples are given to
show that religious literalism and scientific empiricism share many
of the same psychological characteristics. It is argued that our
experience of the division of religion into irreconcilable ideologies
has destroyed the common ground upon which individuals could
previously share their private spiritual experiences. An
increasingly secular approach to religion has tended to treat God
and humanity in more and more external terms. It is concluded
that questions such as the existence of God, or the nature of the
human soul, can only be correctly understood in terms of inner
human experience.

Part One

....

MODERN MYTHS

1. The Scientific Revolution and the Modern Mind

A theory was published midway through the sixteenth century that has come to symbolize more than any other the dethronement of the pre-modern era and the ushering in of a new one. It is regarded as a watershed in the history of mankind, and hailed as one of the greatest of our intellectual achievements, and yet when it came it passed by relatively unnoticed. For Nicholas Copernicus, inciting intellectual revolution was certainly far from his mind; still less did he intend to provide a theory that would in time be used to weaken the authority of the ecclesiastical order that he had faithfully and diligently served all his life. Yet this is how posterity remembers him. The theory of this Polish canon of the Catholic Church, which involved putting the sun rather than the earth at the centre of our universe, was only to gain widespread recognition more than a hundred years later. Even then, the seeds of this revolution were planted in the minds of a mere handful of devotees who were inspired by the new vision, despite the overwhelming indifference of the majority and the fierce opposition of a few.

The popular modern image of the Copernican revolution is that it was a movement to replace an inherently religious world-view with a scientific one. From this perspective, the Copernican revolution not only displaced humankind from the centre of the physical universe but also administered the first of a series of blows to our moral self-centredness. The Copernican revolution is a powerful metaphor for the psychological impact of modern science. The psychologist Sigmund Freud argued that what he called the 'universal narcissism of men, their self-love' had suffered 'three blows from the researches of science'. The first was from Copernicus, who had shown that the earth was not at the centre of the universe; the second from Darwin, who had indicated that 'man is not a being different from animals or superior to them'; and thirdly, rather immodestly, Freud claimed that his own theory of the subconscious had shown 'that ego is not master in its own house'.[19] According to this view, modern science is a rival to the traditional religious world-view. This position has sometimes been referred to as the 'warfare thesis' between science and religion, and was most popular at the time Freud wrote the above words, at the turn of the century.[20] It still echoes a popular sentiment in today's secular societies. Progress in science, from the warfare-thesis point of view, is strongly dependent on its being freed from religion. There are many examples that can be cited to support such a view. The numerous conflicts between Christian ideology and scientific advances over the past 300 years appear to support it. These conflicts took place over the Copernican theory itself, the nature of comets, the age of the earth, biological evolution, and so on – the list is considerable.

Bertrand Russell, another advocate of the 'warfare thesis' who has written much on the historical conflict between the Church and scientific discovery, comments on the significance of seventeenth-century science for the modern world as follows: 'Almost everything that distinguishes the modern world is attributable to science, which achieved its most spectacular triumphs in the seventeenth century'.[21] Russell, in his book *Religion and Science*, describes the Copernican revolution as 'the first pitched battle between theology and science'.[22]

The shift from an earth-centred cosmology to a sun-centred one, according to the warfare thesis, began a shift away from the medieval religious world-view towards the modern scientific one, away from spiritual salvation as the central concern of humanity, towards the objective description of nature as a prime goal.

The medieval universe, so poetically described by Dante, was a universe where humanity's moral salvation was objectively overlaid onto the physical cosmos. This pre-Copernican universe had the earth at its centre surrounded by the concentric orbits of the moon, the sun and the stars. Heaven was located beyond the ninth celestial orbit, and inner concentric rings within the earth converged on hell. Humanity's spiritual salvation was mapped onto this cosmology: if a person chose to be a believer, he would rise heavenwards, ascending through the outer celestial rings to abide in blissful peace forever. If he chose to sin, he would take the route down into the earth's core and be tormented eternally in hell. Medieval cosmology reflected man's dual nature as half-angel, half-animal, in the intermediate position he occupied in the physical universe. Humanity stood at the boundary between two universes: the angelic universe above him, and the animal universe below him. For those who interpret history according to the warfare thesis between science and religion, the interdependence of the medieval moral and physical universes meant that when a shift away from an earth-centred universe came, it led inevitably to a shift in the old perspective whereby humanity's spiritual salvation occupied the central position in the moral universe. Like the position of the earth itself, humanity's position in the cosmos began to appear random and accidental. How could we still consider ourselves the entire focus and purpose of creation when the ground beneath our feet appeared to take such an arbitrary position in the universe? Was our position in the moral order also relative and accidental, like the position of the earth in the Copernican universe?

The psychological impact of the Copernican revolution is thus considered by advocates of the warfare thesis between science and religion to strengthen the notion of a universe devoid of purpose. Bertrand Russell, for instance, writes:

But when Copernicus and his successors persuaded the world that it is we who rotate while the stars take no notice of our earth; when it appeared further that our earth is small compared to several of the planets, and that they are small compared to the sun; when calculation and the telescope revealed the vastness of the solar system, of our galaxy, and finally of the universe of innumerable galaxies – it became increasingly difficult to believe that such a remote and parochial retreat could have the importance to be expected of the home of Man, if Man had the cosmic significance assigned to him in traditional theology. Mere considerations of scale suggested that perhaps we were not the purpose of the universe; lingering self-esteem whispered that, if we were not the purpose of the universe, it probably had no purpose at all.[23]

A famous passage from the seventeenth-century French mathematician and physicist Blaise Pascal is often quoted: 'Le silence eternel des espaces infinis m'effraie!' (The eternal silence of those infinite spaces terrifies me).[24] The same haunting feeling of cosmic alienation was also expressed by the nineteenth-century English poet, Alfred Tennyson, when he wrote:

O Priestess in the vaults of Death,
O sweet and bitter in a breath,
What whispers from thy lying lip?
'The stars,' she whispers, 'blindly run.'[25]

But was it really the Copernican revolution that had this effect? Certainly, religion as it used to be conceived, as a drama of salvation, is divorced from modern everyday life. Indeed, it seems that spiritual salvation is a concern that has largely been forgotten in western societies.

But an earth-centred view of the cosmos is not essential to understanding the medieval religious portrait of human nature. The infamous conflict between the Catholic Church and the Copernican theory is often exaggerated. There is much historical evidence to suggest that the Catholic hierarchy was not against the Copernican theory in principle, only slow to accept it. Indeed, this was not an unreasonable approach, since at the time of Galileo's conflict with the Church, the evidence in favour of the theory was not fully established. More reliable evidence for the theory became available in succeeding centuries.[26] It is also interesting to note that just after the dispute, Jesuit priests greatly helped in disseminating the theory.[27]

Johan Kepler, the first major astronomer to support the Copernican theory, gave a religious interpretation to the new sun-based astronomy. He regarded the sun as a symbol of God, and found it perfectly natural for the sun to be at the centre of the universe, reflecting God's dominion.[28] Kepler found that Copernican astronomy cohered more closely with his religious beliefs than the former geocentric theory, and this is true for most of the other pioneers of modern science, such as Galileo, Descartes and Newton, who understood the new science to be uncovering new pathways to God. Studying science was compared to reading the 'Book of Nature', a direct analogy with reading the Book of Revelation.

More fundamental to understanding the traditional religious view of human nature is the concept of making an inner journey, the belief that one is travelling along an inward road fulfilling a life-purpose, that of attaining the presence of God. Inherent in this notion of an inner journey is the idea of spiritual liberation: the freeing of one's true self from the shackles of less important selves. In the Judaic, Christian and Islamic religions, this inner struggle is depicted as that of an angelic nature aspiring to master an animal one. In Buddhism, the goal of the religious quest is to break free from the Wheel of Life, from earthly desires and conflicts, and attain to the perfect, peaceful condition of Nirvana. In Hinduism, the goal of religion is to discover the Atman, the eternal God-like self hidden within the world of Maya, which is a realm dominated by temporal, ephemeral images. In Plato's cave of shadows, spiritual liberation is breaking free of the chains that bind us to the world of the senses, the shadows that deceive us, and discovering a 'Sun' of inner truth. The thread that ties all these spiritual traditions together is the idea of freeing one's true self from its secondary elements. The goal of human existence has always, in one form or another, been portrayed in such terms. Spirituality has primarily been concerned with this existential struggle towards discovery of an inner harmony. It has been understood as relating to our search to find a universal meaning, and it is mainly in this sense that the word 'spiritual' will be used in this text.

The first point to note about the religious portrait of human nature is that it is not well-defined. Religious language about the ineffable spiritual core of human beings is of a poetic kind, and the complete description of human nature is believed to be impossible.

Humanity is understood to be a cosmological mystery of the first order.

The world's major religions have the common feature of regarding the human 'soul' as an inner temple, a sacred place, an inner sanctuary where God communes with His creation. Within every human being, it is believed, one can catch sight, however imperfectly, of God's image.

In the New Testament, it is stated: 'Surely you know that you are God's temple and that God's spirit lives in you' (I Cor. 3:16). In the Gospels, Christ clearly says, 'The Kingdom of God cometh not with observation: Neither shall they say, Lo here! or, lo there! for, behold, the Kingdom of God is within you' (Luke 17:20). In the Qur'án, the same sentiment is expressed: 'We will surely show them Our signs in the world and within themselves' (41:53); 'And We know what his soul whispers within him, and we are nearer to him than the jugular vein' (1:15). An Islamic tradition likens every human being to a universe: 'Dost thou think thyself a puny mortal form, when the universe is folded up within thee?'[29] In Hinduism, the innermost recesses of human nature are seen to mirror the light of God: 'When the mind of the Yogi is in harmony and finds rest in the Spirit within, all restless desires gone, then he is a Yukta, one in God. Then his soul a lamp whose light is steady, for it burns in a shelter where no winds come' (Bhagavad Gita 6:18–19). In Ancient Greek culture, Socrates summarized our goal in life in the famous dictum: 'Know Thyself'.

The 'soul' or 'inner spirit' of human beings can be defined only in terms its effects. Every soul is understood to have the potential for acquiring God-like qualities; it has the capacity to be loving, just, compassionate and wise. The strong intuitions or feelings that emerge out of our conscience are typically identified with the soul. Within the Judaic, Christian and Islamic traditions, for instance, the soul is the source of our sense of justice; it is an in-dwelling force that guides our conduct, an inner moral imperative. In ancient Greek philosophy and in Hinduism, the soul is typically described in terms of an inner balance, a peaceful condition beyond desire and conflict. But beyond matters of inner experience, there is no clear picture of what a soul might be.

The religious portrait of human nature is also founded on the creative power of the mind, and freedom of will is inherent in the religious conception of human nature. Every religion assumes we have an ability to make moral choices, and that our free will, self-knowledge, consciousness, ability to reason and imagine, and the value we put on truth are all founded upon the 'spiritual' self and the journey it is making to fulfil its purpose. All these qualities are regarded as sacred, that is, God-like in character. Their very existence is taken to be a sign that there is a deeper self – a spiritual core to human experience. This moral centre, and not the supposed position of the earth in the universe, is the key to understanding the traditional religious world-view.

A long line of philosophers, theologians and scientists has developed the theme of the unique mystery of the mind. From different perspectives, they have emphasized the creative power of the mind, and demonstrated that every significant aspect of human nature is linked to special qualities of the mind: our ability to make moral choices, our ability to reason, our self-identity, our capacity to be creative, our search for meaning. These mental qualities are pre-existent, and as a result cannot be explained, since all our explanations are based directly upon them. We can never be objective about them since we live within them.

Aristotle emphasized the primary importance of the mind's ability to extract universal truth-categories from a flow of sense perceptions. He gave the example of the fundamental laws of logic, without which there cannot be any form of reasoning: these laws come from our experience, they are creative constructions of the mind, and no amount of reasoning can derive them, since all forms of reasoning must in some way use them. He also developed the theme that a constant self-identity is essential to human knowledge – the person who draws the conclusions from a certain argument cannot be different from the one who started it! Plato emphasized the primary role of an inner intuition of truth: without this sense of truth, and the value placed upon searching for truth, there can be no significant human knowledge. Similarly, without an indwelling sense of justice, there can be no moral life.

Philosophers and theologians in the Middle Ages, working in an Islamic, Judaic or Christian framework, all made similar points. Avicenna, an Islamic philosopher, emphasized the primary role of our ability to reason. Like Descartes centuries later, he took this ability to be one of the more important God-like powers within us, defining our humanity. These intuitions about the essential mystery, uniqueness and power of the mind, are common to all religious descriptions of human nature.

Notions of truth and meaning are also integral to the religious side of human nature. Human beings have an in-built instinct to search for truth and meaning, and every effort made in the search can be seen in the wider context of discovering who we really are. From a religious point of view, all that we experience as meaningful and true is ultimately related. Every truth leads us naturally to discover a deeper truth, and this is the sign of an instinct whose main characteristic is to search for God.

Moral values are woven into the religious picture of humanity's spiritual progress. Along with the idea that human existence is a drama of different selves, each vying with the other to control our actions, comes the notion that there are objects of absolute value. Values of truth, justice, humility, compassion and so on are, from the religious standpoint, all inseparable from the journey towards spiritual liberation.

The impact of modern science on the human self-image is something we are still searching to understand. Some critics of modern scientific attitudes, the psychologist Floyd Matson, the social scientist Theodore Roszak, the biologist Rupert Sheldrake, the physicist Fritjof Capra, the mathematician Alfred Whitehead and many more, claim that contemporary problems with the human self-image are rooted in a world-view that emerged from early seventeenth-century pioneers of modern science.

The Copernican revolution is often cited as the starting point for a progressive dehumanization felt to have occurred over the past 300 years, since the rise of modern science. The term 'dehumanization' suggests the taking away of our ability to reason by suppressing our capacity to make choices; it denotes attempts at understanding human beings entirely in impersonal terms like those used in physics, without taking human reason or feelings into account. If our ability to reason is marginalized, even in theoretical terms, we are dehumanized; imagine, for instance, presenting your reasons for making a certain choice, and obtaining the response that your listener will not even in principle consider them, because he or she knows the real causes behind your actions or choices. Part of the respect we accord to each other involves taking the thinking and choices of other human beings seriously. The assumption that human behaviour and human reasoning are to be understood with reference to physical causes alone is a form of dehumanization.

A diseased brain is often successfully understood in terms of physical causes. But can healthy minds be understood in terms of physical causes alone? If we insist from the outset that human nature is entirely reducible to such terms, we run the risk of unnecessarily treating all human beings as if they were mentally ill.

The following pages deliberately focus on the extreme positions taken in the mind–brain debate. A significant reaction has developed against the mainstream approach of simply assuming that the mind is reducible to brain physiology. The purpose of presenting the extreme positions here is to identify ideology, as opposed to well-reasoned argument or genuine scientific research.

In the seventeenth century, at the very beginnings of modern science, the universe was popularly conceived of as a vast interlocking machine running on the laws of mathematical physics. Floyd Matson writes that the 'mechanization of man' began at this time, when humanity began to be regarded as merely a cog in a grand universal mechanism.[30] Elsewhere he states that this process inevitably led to a 'disintegration of the inner sense of identity' and a 'flight from autonomous conduct to automaton behaviour'.[31] The historian Professor Burtt, in his well-known summary of the psychological impact of Newtonian science on traditional culture, writes that Newton's authority was put

> squarely behind that view of the cosmos which saw in man a puny irrelevant spectator (so far as a being wholly imprisoned in a dark room can be called such) of the vast mathematical system whose regular motions according to mechanical principles constituted the world of nature. . . . The world that people had thought themselves living in – a world rich with colour and sound, redolent with fragrance, filled with gladness, love and beauty, speaking

everywhere of purposive harmony and creative ideals – was crowded now into minute corners in the brains of scattered organic beings. The really important world outside was a world hard, cold, colourless, silent and dead.[32]

Here, human beings are seen as having been pushed out of their former position at a moral centre, to become spectators watching the grand performance of mechanical nature. The point is not simply that nature took centre stage in the cosmos; the real significance in psychological terms is that it displaced human nature. Human beings left the cosmos as subjects, and returned to it as peripheral objects, strangers in a vast teeming system of matter that is indifferent to their thoughts, numb to their aspirations and cold to their passions and loves.

The shattering of the human self-image, many critics allege, came about through the redefinition of reality into measurable, mathematical qualities such as extension, speed, mass and so on, and secondary qualities like colour, smell and texture. The seventeenth-century pioneers of science such as Galileo and Descartes are criticized for proposing such a distinction, which it is claimed has encouraged us to regard human experience as secondary and subjective, while giving primary importance to the world of mechanical or mathematical entities. Professor Burtt identifies the following extract from Galileo's writings as significant in this process:

> But that external bodies, to excite in us these tastes, these odours, and these sounds, demanded other than size, figure, number, and slow or rapid motion, I do not believe; and I judge that, if the ears, the tongue, and the nostrils were taken away, the figure, the numbers, and the motions would indeed remain, but not the odours nor the tastes nor the sounds, which . . . I do not believe are anything else than names.[33]

Burtt says this 'primary–secondary doctrine' is 'a fundamental step toward that banishing of man from the great world of nature and his treatment as an effect of what happens in the latter'.[34]

Whitehead has called this division 'a fallacy of misplaced concreteness'.[35]

Capra and Sheldrake point out that the division between the human subject and an impersonal nature was given a philosophical foundation in the work of Descartes. They claim that Descartes, by regarding all but the soul of a human being as mechanical, divided the universe unnecessarily into mind and body. Capra quotes Descartes as stating that 'there is nothing included in the concept of body that belongs to the mind; nothing in that of mind that belongs to the body'.[36] The philosopher William Barret likens Descartes' mind–body distinction to a 'Christian soul that has undergone another crucifixion: this time on the cross of mathematical physics'.[37] Here, Descartes' philosophy of mind is interpreted as implying the existence of an unbridgeable divide between human beings as subjects – separate, isolated egos – and the rest of the cosmos. For the critics of the modern impersonal world-view, the so-called 'Cartesian Divide' is a crucial step in alienating humanity from the cosmos; it has been referred to by another philosopher, Gilbert Ryle, as a philosophy based on the existence of a 'ghost in a machine'.[38]

But a word in defence of Galileo and Descartes is appropriate here. Neither Galileo nor Descartes were proposing a 'primary–secondary doctrine' suggesting that the human mind was secondary and mathematical qualities were primary. Like most other seventeenth-century scientists they pointed out the limitations of the empirical qualities of nature, as compared with its underlying mathematical properties. Descartes, for example, gave the example of a straight stick appearing to be bent when half-immersed in water. Galileo and Descartes indicated that empirical information taken by itself can be misleading, just as optical illusions can deceive our eyes. They believed that empirical knowledge was only part of the truth, whereas the mathematical properties of nature provided a more reliable way of studying the world.

They were, therefore, emphasizing the power of the mind. To use a modern philosophical term, they were 'rationalists' in the spirit of say Plato or Aristotle. Rationalist philosophy focuses on the power of the mind, especially its ability to discover the mathematical qualities of nature, in contrast to the limitations of information-gathering by the senses.

Even a superficial reading of Descartes' philosophy reveals that he was primarily concerned with demonstrating the creative power of the mind. Descartes' search for the most fundamental of all truths, one that could not be doubted, even in principle, led him to the conclusion that all knowledge was based on two fundamental truths of our experience. The first was the primacy of the mind: 'I think, therefore I am', since the very process of doubting our thinking will itself inevitably involve us in thinking. The second was the concept of God. Descartes emphasized that the guidance of God lay at the foundation of all knowledge, which linked the mind to the rest of the world. He realized that the mind by itself was intrinsically helpless; there is no guarantee that our thoughts about the world or about ourselves are meaningful. Knowledge, as well as being based on special characteristics of the mind, such as its capacity to think, also depends, according to Descartes, upon God: 'The first and principal intuitive truth . . . is that there is a God upon whom all depend.'.[39] Rather than describing Descartes' philosophy in terms of a 'ghost in a machine', it may be more accurately summarized by the phrase 'God in a machine'!

Descartes' philosophy does not imply the existence of a mental world completely severed from the rest of the cosmos, as suggested by many of his modern critics. This conclusion derives from a secular reading of Descartes' work, a reading that filters out the role of God as the unifying component in his philosophy. In Descartes' own mind, the world of God acted as a bridge between human minds and the rest of the cosmos. Descartes' philosophy is essentially tripartite in character, and not dualist.

The notion that traditional approaches to human nature were 'dualist' is a result of a common secular bias within modern philosophy. Other traditional philosophies that are often supposed to rely on a dualist approach to human nature are in fact tripartite in character. This is as true for the ancient Greeks like Plato (whose philosophy is nearly always cited as the prime example of dualism), as it is for the spiritual traditions that derive from the world's major religions. In all these traditions, an inner experience of God is seen to unite the world of the mind with the rest of the cosmos.

Critics of the modern impersonal world-view however do have a point. Although it is unjustified to attribute the 'primary–secondary doctrine' to seventeenth-century scientists, it is nevertheless an influential strand in modern thought. Exactly why is a complex issue. Our view of ourselves cannot be separated from our view of the universe, and our human self-portrait today has grown out of three centuries of rapid change, not just in science, but also in religion and philosophy.

Critics have also accused Descartes of propagating a philosophy of 'reductionism'. This refers to the method of analytical reasoning that breaks down complex phenomena into their component parts, then reorders them in a way that is easier to understand and use. It is a line of thinking analogous to reducing a complex machine to its component parts; reductionism proceeds as if the phenomena under study can be regarded as no more than a linear sum of their individual elements. This method has become an integral part of science since the seventeenth century, and as a methodology has proved to be astoundingly successful in scientific research. But according to its critics, it has also fostered a wider attitude of reductionism outside the narrow confines of mechanical science in which it grew, which is now used when working with phenomena that naturally resist simple methodological dissection. The result, according to the critics of reductionism, is a distortion or misrepresentation of the original phenomena: the creation of multiplicity where there was previously a natural unity. Fritjof Capra writes that reductionism has 'led to the fragmentation that is characteristic of both our general thinking and academic disciplines'.[40] Reductionism, according to Roszak, is responsible for 'the turning of people and nature into worthless things'.[41] The writer and poet Kathleen Raine says that reductionism is the kind of thinking that would have us 'see in the pearl nothing but a disease of the oyster'.[42]

Again, the critics of modern impersonal science have a point. But it is not at all clear where the tendency towards reductionism comes from. In a sense, there is a tendency for scientists in any age to be reductionist: it is tempting to squeeze all our experience into terms that fit the latest theories about the universe. It was natural for seventeenth-century scientists to view the cosmos according to principles of classical physics; Descartes' statement 'Give me extension and I will construct the universe'[43] is clearly to be understood in this context. But seventeenth-century scientists did not reduce everything to mechanistic terms. Descartes, for example, showed that he could not reduce the world of the mind or the concept of God to anything simpler. For Descartes, these were the most fundamental of all building blocks upon which the world of nature and human nature were founded. In other words, seventeenth-century scientists understood their science to have limits. They were enthusiastic about their science as are scientists in every age, but were careful not to weigh everything in its balances.

Another important point to bear in mind when understanding the work of these scientists is that they looked upon the whole of science as their own individual project. Science was a personal venture that could be 'owned' by a small number of intellectuals. Descartes considered that, helped by God, he had discovered a universal secret, one based upon the intuition that mathematics was the key to understanding the universe. The history of modern science has of course confirmed that this intuition is a very powerful one. The insight came to Descartes in a series of dreams, which he himself interpreted to be mystical in character. The notion that the world of nature has underlying mathematical properties was not new; Pythagoras said 2,500 years ago that 'all things are numbers'. Yet Descartes understood mathematics to be only a part of something much larger. 'All philosophy is like a tree,' he wrote. 'The roots are metaphysics, the trunk is physics, and the branches are all the other sciences.'[44]

Descartes was no reductionist; he did not try to explain human wisdom (metaphysics) in terms of physics, as was attempted by others in succeeding centuries. Among the 'maxims' that Descartes presented before describing his famous philosophical observations in the *Discourse on Method* is the resolution to 'conquer myself rather than fortune, to change my desires rather than the order of the world'.[45] This suggests that Descartes placed more importance on self-knowledge than on a mechanistic understanding of nature.

Sheldrake, Capra and Sherrad all regard Francis Bacon, a seventeenth-century philosopher, as advocating a philosophy based on the exploitation of nature. They support this view by quoting statements of Francis Bacon about nature being 'forced out of her natural state and squeezed and moulded'.[46] Bacon's aim in science is said to have been that 'human knowledge and human power meet as one'.[47] Science therefore becomes a pursuit to acquire wisdom in order to practise manipulation. The scientific utopias of the seventeenth century, which Bacon himself so vividly portrayed (he envisaged the creation of a new Atlantis based on the principles of the new science), are characterized by Roszak as a vision of total scientific domination – an ideology based on the promise of total power.[48]

These criticisms about the relationship between modern science and human values are important. There is now a gulf between scientific knowledge and traditional wisdom, a separation between facts and values. But is modern science itself at fault, or does the problem relate to its proper application? Many writers this century have warned of the dangers of losing sight of our humanity in a technocratic society. But has this danger really been brought upon us by the philosophy of the seventeenth-century pioneers of modern science? Descartes, as quoted above, sought to 'conquer' himself rather than change the 'order of the world'. Francis Bacon was not a scientist, but a popularizer of science. He did not make any direct contributions to the development of modern science. He differed from the pioneers of modern science in that he thought science could be reduced to simple rules that anyone could follow; his credentials for representing the philosophy of seventeenth-century scientists are at best debatable. Moreover, the criticisms levelled at Bacon do not take account of his fervent prayer:

I humbly pray, that things human may not interfere with things divine, and that from the opening of the ways of sense and the increase of natural light there may arise in our minds no incredulity or darkness with regard to divine mysteries; but rather that the understanding [is] thereby purified and purged of fancies and vanity. . . . Lastly

knowledge . . . which makes the mind of man to swell, we
may not be wise above measure and sobriety, but cultivate
truth and charity.[49]

Roszak quotes this prayer as an example of a contradiction in
Bacon's philosophy. But is this really a fair interpretation? Was
Bacon not like many of his contemporaries who, although they
speculated about the great advances science would make, still
prayed that it would always serve traditional wisdom? What has
changed in the centuries that separate us from Bacon is our reorientation as regards traditional wisdom. At the time of Bacon,
there was a general consensus about what was wise. It was based
upon a religious moral imperative, such as: 'What shall it profit a
man if he gain the whole world, and lose his own soul?' Today,
there is no clear reason why 'knowledge' should not make 'the
mind of man to swell', and indeed, no reason why knowledge
should not be pursued for its own sake, or used in an attempt to
'gain the whole world'.

The separation between facts and values did not exist in the
seventeenth century. There were of course, great hopes for the new
science, but it was considered to be a tree rooted in metaphysical,
indeed mystical ground. There was a balance between science and
religion that no longer exists. Before all else, there was the
question of the human soul and its journey towards God. Moral
values, in relation to the spiritual nature of humanity and our life
purpose, were considered to be primary, while scientific knowledge
was secondary; in other words the world of human nature was
primary in relation to the world of nature. This, in a nutshell, was
the 'primary–secondary doctrine' of the seventeenth century,
shared by all the great founders of modern science.

2. Hume and the Rise of Empiricism

In the eighteenth century, the so-called Age of Reason, seventeenth-century science, principally Newtonian science, was taken as the founding inspiration of the Enlightenment movement. Inextricably linked to this movement was the rise of empiricism, a philosophy that extended Newton's experimental method to subjects outside the domain of physics. The spirit of empiricism underlay much popular thinking about the nature of humanity throughout the nineteenth and twentieth centuries. The writings of the eighteenth-century Scottish philosopher and historian David Hume capture this mood. The subtitle to one of his famous philosophical works (*Treatise of Human Nature*) declared the ambitious objective shared by many contemporary thinkers, to 'Introduce the Experimental Method of Reasoning into Moral Subjects'. Hume aimed at founding a science of human nature – he conceived it to be a 'moral science'. Hume's philosophy raises many questions still unresolved in the modern mind. In some ways, his philosophy foreshadows the many inconsistencies and fragmentations of modern thought.

Hume's method was to give priority to the senses, which he believed cohered in human beings according to a principle of association, much as objects in the physical world were brought together through gravitational attraction. Hume claimed that the varied experiences of the mind could be explained by describing association to be 'a kind of attraction, which in the mental world will be found to have as extraordinary effects as in the natural, and to show itself in as many and as various forms'.[50]

Hume modelled the mind as a constant stream of sense

impressions, distinct and separate like atoms of consciousness. The 'I' or the 'Self', it was postulated, was nothing but a changing heap of sensations. In Hume's philosophy, the unitary experience of personal identity, with its uniqueness and its self-awareness, disintegrates along a flow of changing perceptions. There is no room for self-knowledge, self-examination, or self-identity in Hume's philosophy. One is left with the paradoxical task of seeking to know oneself by looking outward, to one's experience of the outside world: to a flow of sense-data.

There is no fixed personality in Hume's philosophy. 'For my part', writes Hume, 'when I enter most intimately into what I call myself, I always stumble on some particular perception or other, of heat or cold, light or shade.'[51] This strict empirical test to determine self-knowledge may be likened to a man going outside his house to peer through the window and check whether he is in the house or not! One might ask who it is that catches the self observing 'some particular perception or other'! There is surely an infinite regress involved here, down which the self inexorably retreats. Self-knowledge is defeated by an infinite chain of perceptions: a set of perceptions observes another set of perceptions, which themselves are being observed by yet another set . . . and so on. If there is no mind anchoring all these perceptions together, the self becomes an illusion.

Hume describes the mind as an anarchic theatre of mingling perceptions:

> The mind is a kind of theatre, where several perceptions successively make their appearance; pass, re-pass, glide away, and mingle in an infinite variety of postures and situations. There is properly no simplicity in it at one time, nor identity.[52]

It is as if our minds are dimly lit, empty stages that carry only the images, lights and sounds of the external world. The 'universe within' is a dark realm; our memories, thoughts, hopes and feelings, which all cohere in us to create an identifiable experience, a unique personality of our own, for Hume only amount to the illusion of a single experience and do not properly belong to us. According to Hume, our minds are puppets of the senses and we are composed of many unrelated, constantly changing selves. The lingering self-defeat inherent in such a proposition is not seriously discussed by Hume.

He was one of the first to formulate an empirical approach to the mind, rebelling against the traditional view of the mind as the theatre of a spiritual and moral drama. Ever since the eighteenth century, the philosophy of mind has been characterized by this type of empirical approach, and its overall aims echo Hume's intention of making his philosophy a strictly 'scientific' one.

A philosophy based on giving priority to the senses sets the tone for the pattern of modern life. We are constantly bombarded by images and sounds aimed at shaping our desires and thoughts; advertising companies and the media depend on this. The consumer society is based on a belief that people's minds are primarily governed by their senses, and consumerism is founded on the premiss that if people see and hear about a certain product for long enough, they will eventually begin to desire it. Appeals are made to the senses, and not to reason. An individual in modern society is constantly subjected to different 'perceptions' emanating from the external world, each vying with the other not just to inform us, but to mould us.

Another area in which Hume articulated much that is characteristic of modern thinking was in his scepticism about postulating theories on anything beyond so-called observable 'facts'. Here Hume's scepticism leads him to assert not only the primacy of facts, but the characteristically modern idea that they must be 'brute facts': that is, facts without any ultimate rationale or purpose behind them. Hume's scepticism goes so far that he even doubts the notion of causality and the existence of a world external to our minds, two beliefs upon which science, obviously, is founded. Hume's scepticism is taken to the point of self-defeat: he sets out to construct a science of human nature, and ends by doubting the validity of science itself. Very few philosophers after him were able to maintain such an extreme form of scepticism, but by adopting the spirit of Hume's scepticism their own philosophies suffer from a certain inconsistency.

The philosophy of Bertrand Russell, for example, has been

influential in our own century. Russell has contributed greatly to philosophy, and there is much of immense value in his work, especially his spirit of independent enquiry unobtruded by social or cultural prejudices. Russell's philosophy, at its best, is an inspirational example of free thinking. Yet there are weaknesses in it. Russell draws much from Hume's scepticism in his notion that the universe is a brute fact. In a debate with the theologian and philosopher Frederick Copleston, Russell said: 'I should state the universe is just there, and that's all.'[53] The mysteries underlying science are marginalized by such a statement. Science is implicitly founded on the belief in a chain of causes, with each cause preceded in some sense by a more profound one; it is based on a search for unity in the universe, a search for universal truths, and this presupposes that there is something meaningful to discover. What is it that makes science worthy of our attention? In a universe without meaning, are not all forms of human activity, in the final analysis, also meaningless? Why place any value on science? Indeed, why place any value on anything? Why set out on a road that leads nowhere? For Russell, the universal truths uncovered by science are somehow exempt from being meaningless. He made it clear that scientific investigation was, for him, a meaningful search to uncover deeper and deeper causes in the universe. Not only did scientific enquiry involve some notion of universal meaning, but it was regarded as the only legitimate form of enquiry. Russell stated: 'Whatever can be known, can be known by means of science.'[54]

This contradiction within Russell's philosophy is not an uncommon one in modern thinking. At first glance, denying the universe any ultimate meaning might seem unrelated to our faith in science. Yet when the situation is examined more closely, it is not at all clear why science, a form of enquiry based on discovering universal truths, should retain meaning in a universe without universal truths. There is no refuge from scepticism in simply asking what we mean by meaning – a question that of course rings with paradox. It is not at all clear how we can compartmentalize our notion of meaning. Rejection of ultimate meanings and assertions that the universe comprises brute facts, undermines science and robs it of its background vision – in effect, turning it into a series of techniques and procedures.

It might be suggested Russell's statement that the 'universe is just there, and that's all' can be better understood in terms of seeking to advance human knowledge; Russell had respect for science as providing human meaning, as something quite distinct from an unknowable universal meaning. That may be Russell's approach, but it has some contradictions within it. If science is to be understood in terms of providing human knowledge of universal truths, was Copleston, who put forward a theological picture of the universe, not also concerned with that goal? Is not religion also about the pursuit of human knowledge about universal truths? We cannot monopolize truth by stating that its only valid forms are those that come from scientific investigation.

But there is a deeper contradiction. Whether the route be through religion or through science, a universal truth must by its very nature link together all other forms of truth. The statement 'the universe is just there, and that's all' discourages us from setting out on any road to find universal truth because it implies that such truths do not exist. It decides the outcome before any investigation is made, and is in this sense a closed philosophical position, incompatible with the spirit underlying both science and religion. This is a common contradiction in modern thinking, which in other instances prides itself on its openness.

The nature of Hume's strict empiricism can be further understood by studying his rejection of any kind of knowledge that is not reducible to either 'fact or figure'. In order to distinguish between real and apparent knowledge, Hume proposes a test that he believes distinguishes truth from falsehood. This test is known as 'Hume's Fork', and it later inspired many other attempts at designing criteria for truth. Hume here describes the application of this test in evaluating what is traditionally regarded as metaphysical knowledge:

When we run over libraries persuaded of these principles, what havoc must we make? If we take in our hand any volume; of divinity or school metaphysics, for instance; let us ask, Does it contain any abstract reasoning concerning quantity or number? No. Does it contain any experimental

reasoning concerning matter of fact or existence? No.
Commit it then to the flames: for it can contain nothing
but sophistry and illusion.[55]

Hume's Fork is an influential strand of thought in the modern
mind, although it must be admitted that few thinkers can be found
today who confidently apply it in the form recommended above.
Yet it captures a strand in modern psychology that tends to dismiss
the non-factual or the non-mathematical as unscientific. It reflects
the prevalent mood advocating rejection of non-observable, non-
quantifiable aspects of our experience, believing them to be less
important than what can be directly observed and quantified.

The wider implications of such a criterion for truth are not
usually pursued; its naturally self-defeating characteristics are not
highlighted. What, for instance, are we to make of Hume's Fork
itself: does it contain abstract reasoning concerning quantity or
number? No. Does it contain any experimental reasoning
concerning matter of fact? No. Commit it then to the flames: for it
can contain nothing but sophistry and illusion!

But there are many other problems in using such a simple test
as a criterion to distinguish truth from falsehood. Where do human
values, such as justice or compassion, fit into this test? Hume
cannot find a place in his empirical system for values which, he
says, lie outside reason's capacity to affirm. "'Tis not contrary to
reason to prefer the destruction of the whole world to the
scratching of my fingers."[56] Yet Hume's philosophy enjoins the
pursuit of ethics. He merely makes the theoretical distinction
between fact and value, and in practice prescribes an ethical life –
ironically borrowing much from the religious outlook of his
period.[57]

There is much in modern thought that is characteristic of such
a fact–value distinction. Hume points to the limitation of human
reason, and in its stead recommends experience as a much surer
foundation not only for enquiries into knowledge, but also for
understanding how to live. Hume maintains that just like reason,
ethics and values are matters of habit, part of the principles of
human nature. In practice, this means that we should 'follow our
instincts'.

There is clearly a divorce between experience and theory in
Hume's philosophy. He does not recommend following the
sceptical conclusions at which he arrives, and advocates
'carelessness and inattention' in trying to avoid its alienating
consequences in everyday living.

> This sceptical doubt, both with respect to reason and the
> senses is a malady, which can never be radically cured, but
> must return upon us every moment, however we may chase
> it away, and sometimes may seem entirely free from it . . .
> carelessness and inattention alone can afford us any
> remedy.[58]

Here Hume is recommending faith – a faith in the experience of
living – as an antidote to the conclusions of his own scepticism. It
is a curious inconsistency when, after formulating his philosophy,
the philosopher advises the reader not to take his conclusions
seriously, and to treat them as 'a malady' that must be chased away
at every possible moment. This is an important inconsistency in
western philosophical thought, although not all Hume's readers
have been so ready to state openly that their sceptical conclusions
were like a 'malady'.

Hume's objective was a positive one. His criticisms of human
reason were made with the purpose of showing it to be limited
with respect to our total experience. The aim of his philosophy was
to alert us to the dangers of becoming preoccupied by mental
abstractions, without reference to our experience. From this
perspective, his work is immensely valuable, and has had a lasting
impact. Ironically, Hume's philosophy relies on faith in human
nature, and faith in our experience. Looked at in this way, his
description of his own conclusions as a 'malady' is not inconsistent.

But there are intrinsic weaknesses. Hume places science in the
straitjacket of empiricism, and the cutting edge of his scepticism
can only be taken so far: that is, up to the point where it threatens
to cut off the branch upon which it sits. Without a Hume-like
faith in human nature to prop it up, the whole edifice of human
thought would come tumbling down.

Hume's philosophy epitomizes the schism between reason and

experience, between reason and faith, between fact and value, and the ideological sway of scientific empiricism over the modern mind. It is based upon giving priority to the senses, a priority that has come to characterize the pattern of life in the modern world, both in theory and in practice. A natural consequence is to view the human mind as a dark, passive place in which all our everyday feelings and beliefs about ourselves slip into an abyss of sense-data.

This kind of empiricism – the desire to apply the experimental methods of Newtonian science to human subjects, the attempt to find quantifiable criteria to describe human nature – was pursued by other philosophers in the eighteenth century, such as those known as the Utilitarians. The Utilitarians are perhaps most well known for modelling human nature on the principle of maximizing happiness: human actions were to be understood in terms of either bringing happiness or failing to do so. Jeremy Bentham, an eighteenth-century philosopher and a leading proponent of the utilitarian approach, conceived happiness to be a mathematical measure of human behaviour, 'a sort of arithmetic of pleasure', a 'felecific calculus'.[59] This was later developed into the notion of the human being as 'pleasure machine': human actions were to be understood in terms of instinctual urges to maximize pleasure and minimize pain.[60]

Like Hume's philosophy, that of the Utilitarians is consistent with today's consumerism and modern advertising practices. People are assumed to be governed primarily by urges to maximize their happiness and pleasure through the acquisition of more and more money, and more and more material comfort. Elaborate marketing strategies are devised based upon the belief that human beings act only in this way. Modern consumerism seems to have become a practical embodiment of eighteenth-century empiricist philosophy.

3. Positivism: The Religion of Science

The empirical movement of the eighteenth century laid the foundation for a philosophy that came to be known as 'positivism', which developed in the late nineteenth and early twentieth centuries. This term was coined by the philosopher Auguste Comte (1798–1857), who interpreted Hume-style empiricism as a veritable *religion* of science. Comte distinguished three stages of human development throughout history. The first was theology, which he defined as the explanation of events in terms of gods and spirits. The second phase he took to be metaphysics, or the explanation of nature in terms of abstract unobservable causes, like Plato's Forms. Finally, the third and most enlightened stage of human development, according to Comte, arrived when explanations about nature were given in terms of observations tested by the methods of science – the third or 'positive' stage of human development was, in effect, the development of modern science.[61]

Comte stressed the exclusiveness of scientific investigation – it was to become the ultimate method of distinguishing truth from falsehood. He envisaged a time when all education would be scientific, and where theology and metaphysics would be abolished. Although it demands the complete negation of metaphysics and theology, this philosophy was described as the 'positive' objective.[62]

Positivist objectives were formulated into an explicit system of philosophy in the 1920s and early 1930s, which was known as logical positivism. Although it is no longer influential as a philosophical school and was relatively short-lived (flourishing between the two world wars), logical positivism does epitomize an important strand in modern thought, particularly in the emphasis it placed on empirical enquiry. The founders of logical positivism combined the positivist doctrines of Hume-type empiricism with the logic formulated early this century by Whitehead and Russell in their three-volume publication, *Principia Mathematica* (1910–13).[63]

The development of this logic grew out of an attempt to solve what became known as the problem of 'consistency in mathematics'. An attempt was made at finding a secure foundation for mathematics, one in which all axioms are clear and explicit, and do not lead to any contradictions.[64] Russell claimed to have solved the problem of consistency through his work on *Principia Mathematica*, which reduced the operations of mathematics to simple steps of deductive logic. Russell concluded that in the final analysis, mathematics was nothing but a tautology; '1+1=2' was only another way of saying 'A=A' or '0=0'. According to this view, mathematical statements were similar to statements such as 'all bachelors are men', and nothing can be new or original in mathematics. It is reduced to a series of logical, mechanical operations.

The founders of the logical positivist philosophy took this new logic as a guiding method of analysing the propositions of philosophy and science. They called all mathematical statements 'analytical' (in the terminology of the eighteenth-century philosopher Kant) because they were believed to be in principle a chain of logical inferences. They claimed that the new logic went hand in hand with science, and provided a philosophy for scientific investigation. It was not regarded as one method among other methods, but as the *only* method of analysis on which all philosophy was to be modelled. The mathematician Rudolf Carnap, an exponent of the positivist school, described it as follows:

Perhaps this method can be briefly characterized as consisting in the logical analysis of the statement and concepts of empirical science. This description indicates the two most important features that distinguish this method from the methods of traditional philosophy. First, this type of philosophizing goes strictly hand in hand with empirical science. Thus, philosophy is no longer viewed as a domain of knowledge in its own right, on a par with, or superior to, the empirical sciences. Secondly, this description indicates the part that philosophy plays in empirical science; more specifically, in the decomposition of statements into their parts (concepts), the step by step reduction of concepts to more fundamental concepts and of statements to more fundamental statements. This way of setting the problem brings out the value of logic for philosophical enquiries. Logic is no longer merely one philosophical discipline among others, but we are able to say outright: Logic is the method of philosophizing.[65]

This quotation emphasizes that the logical positivists saw their method as 'scientific', and regarded it as the measure of all philosophy which, it was believed, should proceed along the lines of deductive logic, drawing step-by-step inferences to arrive at fundamental propositions. This resembles the analytical method attributed to Descartes, an essentially reductionist approach of logical analysis, like reducing a machine to its component parts. Here, the new logic becomes a method of science, and analytical thinking becomes the 'rationality' that is demanded in modern scientific investigation. Today, philosophy based on this kind of analytical train of thought is still associated with a formal method in science, and thought to be distinguished from traditional forms of philosophy by its logical precision and rigour.

The acknowledged aim of the logical positivists was to rid philosophy of metaphysics. They defined a criterion for truth, modelled on Hume's Fork, which divided all propositions into two categories. The first category contained analytical statements, that is tautologies, like those thought to be contained in logic and mathematics. The second category comprised matters of fact, which could be tested by observation and experiment; these were defined as statements that were testable by the methods of empirical science, and they were called, using Kant's terminology, 'synthetic' statements.

Statements belonging to the first category did not have anything to say about the world since they were tautologies, while those in the second category could be proved true or false by the methods of empirical science. The logical positivists called this the Verification Principle, and in effect it classified all statements of truth as either mathematics or empirical science, either analytical or synthetic. The concepts in metaphysics and theology that do not pass this test were: 'therefore mere illusory concepts which are to be rejected from the epistemological viewpoint as well as from the scientific viewpoint'.[66]

The difference between the philosophy of the logical positivists and Hume's philosophy was that logical positivism reduced mathematics to a tautology, and hence considered all statements to be either non-factual (tautological) or factual (empirical), with anything else designated as meaningless. Logical positivists considered mathematics to be a tool for empiricism, and not a supplementary source of knowledge about the world set apart from empirical observations. Another important difference between their philosophy and Hume's was that they set out a serious programme aimed at eliminating metaphysics and theology by applying the Verification Principle to the traditional subjects of philosophy. Unlike Hume, after formulating their philosophy they recommended its rigorous use. The logical positivists saw theirs as a crusade for 'decontaminating' science and philosophy from the influence of metaphysics and theology. In the words of Rudolf Carnap:

> With the aid of the rigorous methods of the new logic, we can treat science to a thoroughgoing process of decontamination. Every sentence of science must be proved to be meaningful by logical analysis. If it is discovered that the sentence in question is either a tautology or a contradiction (negation of a tautology), the statement belongs to the domain of logic including mathematics. Alternatively the sentence has factual content, ie, it is neither tautological nor contradictory; it is then an empirical sentence. It is reducible to the given and can, therefore, be discovered, in principle, to be either true

or false. The (true or false) sentences of the empirical sciences are of this character. There are no questions which are in principle unanswerable.[67]

The programme of the logical positivists was, then, one aimed at eliminating all other philosophies, and an attempt at a scientific definition of meaning. By postulating that science revolved around empirical enquiry and sanctioning only deductive (reductionist) chains of reasoning, it could state that 'there are no questions which are in principle unanswerable'. This notion is influential in the modern mind: the notion that in principle, if not in practice, empirical science can discover everything meaningful that is to be found, and that there are no mysteries that cannot be solved. This is explicit in the programme of logical positivists, but is implicit in much of the psychology of the modern mind.

Today, there is a widespread belief, conscious or unconscious, that the methods of science and logic can, in principle, solve any problem worth solving. Since questions such as the existence of God lie outside the realm of empirical science, they are somehow considered less urgent, less significant. The positivist universe has boundaries clearly defined by empirical observations and logical procedures, leaving no room for anything else. It is a philosophy based upon rejecting the mysterious; it is a reductionist programme on a cosmic scale. 'Scientists', it has been said, 'hate mysteries'.[68] This attitude, that the mystery must be taken out of our universe – indeed out of everyday living – is associated with the scientific method, and is characteristic of modern thinking.

The consequences of logical positivism for the study of metaphysics, theology and ethics were spelled out by Alfred J. Ayer in his book *Language, Truth and Logic*. After stating that a proposition should in principle be empirically verifiable, Ayer concludes:

If a putative proposition fails to satisfy this principle, and is not a tautology, then I hold that it is metaphysical, and that, being metaphysical, it is neither true or false, but literally senseless. It will be found that much of what ordinarily passes for philosophy is metaphysical according to this criterion, and in particular, that it can not be significantly asserted that there is a non-empirical world of values, or that men have immortal souls, or that there is a transcendent God.[69]

Here, Ayer defines the 'metaphysical' as anything that does not pass the test of the Verification Principle, and spells out the verdict of logical positivism on theology and ethics: belief in God or in moral values is 'literally senseless'. Logical positivism takes on the responsibility of defining what has meaning and what is meaningless – and most significantly, its authority for doing so is claimed to rest on methods derived from science. Belief in justice, compassion or honesty become nothing more than a department of psychology and sociology.[70]

Ayer develops a so-called 'emotive theory of values', in which values are considered to be mere expressions of feeling, having no objective factual content:

> If now I generalise my previous statement and say, 'Stealing money is wrong', I produce a sentence which has no factual meaning – It is as if I had written 'Stealing money!!' – where the shape and the thickness of the exclamation marks show, by a suitable convention, that a special sort of moral disapproval is the feeling which is being expressed. It is clear that there is nothing said here which can be true or false.[71]

It is important to note that this distinction between fact and value is not simply one that sets values apart from facts; it also implies that values are 'senseless', and are part of a metaphysics that should be eliminated. The title of Ayer's first chapter in *Language, Truth and Logic* is 'The Elimination Of Metaphysics'. Having rejected moral values on the grounds of their inability to pass the verification test, logical positivism demotes them to the status of 'pseudo-concepts'.[72] Although today few people would unequivocally dismiss moral values as senseless, there is an unmistakable tendency to play down their importance. The reasons for doing so, whether conscious or unconscious, are often

related to the objections formulated by the logical positivists, and
rooted in a desire to give priority to empirical scientific enquiry
and a methodology based on logic.

There is no need to dwell on the many inconsistencies of
logical positivism, which led to its abandonment as a formal
philosophy. The Verification Principle itself is a good example.
What happens if one applies the Verification Principle to itself? Is
it a tautology with no factual content? No self-respecting logical
positivist would answer this question in the affirmative.
Alternatively, is it a matter of fact, which can be tested by some
empirical method, such as observation perhaps? The answer here
must again be no, at least not in the way intended in the writings
of logical positivism's founders. Hence, one can only conclude that
it is a piece of mere metaphysics, which is 'senseless' and should be
eliminated.

Another blow for logical positivist philosophy came with the
discovery that mathematics is not at all a succession of deductive
logical inferences. There is a natural incompleteness to the whole
of arithmetic and mathematics, which proves the opposite of what
Principia Mathematica had set out to achieve. This insight was
discovered by Kurt Godel in 1931, at around the time the founders
of logical positivism were formulating their philosophy. Godel
showed that one cannot anticipate the whole domain of
arithmetical truth from a single set of axioms.[73] The conclusion is
that mathematics and arithmetic are not a succession of logic
inferences; there will always be genuine truths of arithmetic that
lie outside a given number of logic-axioms, and which one can
only examine by adopting wider axioms encompassing the
inconsistencies found in the original system. Godel's theory
showed that a formalized deductive procedure, such as the one set
out in *Principia Mathematica*, is always limited by its axioms. In
other words, mathematics is not like a simple look-up table that
can be derived by mechanically applying a set of logical rules. It is
infinitely more creative than a mere tautology, and completely
new discoveries occur in mathematics that are not the outcome of
logical inference, but of intuition. Godel's theory itself is an
astounding demonstration of this very principle. It could not have
been derived out of anything found in *Principia Mathematica*.

New discoveries in mathematics do not rely solely on chains of logical reasoning, but require the intuitive, creative mental leap that finds new axioms. It is not a process one can describe in a formal sense as it is intrinsically non-rational, but it is as much a part of mathematics as using deductive chains of logic.

The notion that mathematics is a tautology comes from giving priority to mechanical operations. It is the result of mechanistic thinking – a consequence of mistaking car-manual science for real science. But it is a notion that is influential in modern thought, which tends to attach more importance to techniques or methodologies than to intuition or imagination. It can be seen in the widespread belief that philosophical concepts can be analysed by logical methods, or that there is a distinctively logical way of communicating that is somehow more scientific than others. This kind of logical precision, however, often takes away more than it gains. When applied to language, metaphysics, religion and even mathematics, it can result in bland reductionism with only a semblance of scientific rigour.

These objections, and many others, brought about the demise of logical positivism as a coherent school of philosophy. Even some of its founders, such as Alfred J. Ayer, later admitted that it was not clearly formulated.[74] For a philosophy that aimed to arrive at strict clarity of philosophical language, there is an obvious irony here.

But the spirit of logical positivism is still very much alive. Recently, Ayer stated that he still considered the future role of philosophy lay 'in its being the logic of science'.[75] The search for a truly 'scientific' philosophy still continues. Bryan Magee, a philosopher who has helped enormously in making philosophy more accessible to the general public, remarked in the 1970s: 'My impression is that even today, in the 1970s, a lot of people – well educated but not educated in philosophy – are under the impression that contemporary philosophy is logical positivism.'[76]

Logical positivism may have ceased to be a formal philosophical school of thought, but it still exercises influence over modern thought. The many difficulties and inconsistencies associated with prescribing a logical method for science, attributing precision to a certain style of philosophical discourse where there is none, and insisting that priority be given to empirical observations irrespective of context, remain unresolved in the largely positivist, modern, western world-view.

4. Behaviourism

While the logical positivists admitted to being part of a philosophical movement (if only just), others were carrying out a programme aimed at decontaminating science from metaphysics, working within science itself. Here the impersonal attitude implicit in the positivist programme was pushed to an even more extreme conclusion. It was most explicitly articulated by the behaviourist school of psychology, which developed around the same time as logical positivism in the early part of the twentieth century.

The image of humanity put forward by behaviourism has been dubbed the 'ratomorphic' view. This name derives from the fact that many of the experiments used in behaviourist studies were performed by controlled stimulation of white rats, and the monitoring of their responses. Human behaviour, according to this school of psychology, could only be understood in terms of behavioural responses to external stimuli.

The founding fathers of behaviourism regarded their approach to human nature as entirely empirical, restricted their study to observable behaviour and eschewed all reference to mental entities such as consciousness, will, values and so on. Behaviourism owes much to the empirical world-view of Hume and the positivism of the logical positivists, yet it must be stressed that it is in one sense significantly different: behaviourists regarded themselves as scientists, not philosophers. Behaviourism is, ironically, a school of psychology that rejected the very term 'psychology', that is, the study of the soul.

The behaviourist school achieved a certain notoriety by

rejecting the concept of free will, which they did in the name of scientific method. In the words of B. F. Skinner, a leading behaviourist, 'the hypothesis that man is not free is essential to the application of the scientific method to the study of human behaviour'.[77] The behaviourists' rejection of human freedom and values was made in the Copernican spirit of dislodging humanity from a moral centre and replacing it with impersonal nature. Behaviourists saw themselves as continuing the trend of earlier centuries: 'It has always been the unfortunate task of science to dispossess cherished beliefs regarding the place of man in the cosmos.'[78]

Rejection of free will was considered essential to the scientific study of human behaviour, but what is unscientific about assuming that human beings have free will? Science was pitched against cherished beliefs about humanity's place in the cosmos, but is there any compelling reason for this? Are there not times when science might equally confirm our most cherished cosmological beliefs? Can science indeed say anything directly about our place in the cosmos? The behaviourists did not attempt to answer these kinds of questions. The perceived link between the scientific method and rejection of free will or of human cosmological beliefs is more psychological than explicitly philosophical or scientific. For the empirically minded, science is simply assumed to entail these impersonal factors.

Implicit in this conception of science is a view that it is largely dominated by mechanistic causes, like those that were thought to operate between objects in classical physics. As a founding principle of science, humanity is assumed to be an object that does not differ fundamentally from other objects. Behaviourists understood objective science to involve the rejection of the creative power of human thought, or the filtering out of all reference to human mental qualities.

The psychology of empirical science is highly influential. Since the process of scientific investigation is regarded by the modern mind as the archetype of all modes of reasoning and thinking, it is not surprising to find that the notion of being 'objective' in an impersonal sense is an ideal that pervades modern western culture. But the psychology behind the concept of impersonal objectivity is a curious one: it seems to revolve around separating oneself from the object under analysis. Now, this approach has obvious merit in certain instances, for example one cannot model the trajectory of a projectile on human actions and purposes. This, as we were constantly reminded by the behaviourists, would be anthropomorphic, seeing the world around us in terms of human traits, which is clearly a mistake. We cannot describe the trajectory of a stone as if it possessed human intentions and purposes. But on the other hand it is equally misguided to treat people in the terms one uses to describe stones. The pursuit of objectivity, in this limited empirical, mechanistic sense, in our relationships with people is obviously dehumanizing. Instead of being able to share experiences with one another, people would have superficial, spectator-type relationships. If the objective ideal were translated into the domain of human relationships it would encourage people to treat each other in a distant manner, with everyone constantly evaluating the utterances and actions of everyone else, as if plotting the trajectory of a stone – without allowing any shared experience to take place. As an ideal in human relationships, objectivity is a negative, anti-social element in our culture, diametrically opposed to community spirit and detrimental to human self-knowledge. It tends to produce individualistic attitudes, where people become emotionally detached and play the role of self-appointed critics in human affairs, oblivious to the fact that they share much with the object under critical examination.

Is it really fair to imply that western culture has translated the notion of impersonal objectivity, borrowed from empirical science, into a model for human relationships? The behaviourists' position is an extreme one, and few people share it in the form in which they expressed it. But if science is conceived of as having an explicit method, and if objectivity is understood to be the foundation stone upon which it rests, then there will be a natural tendency for people to apply this method even in their relationships, since there is no definite line dividing science from non-science.

The ideal of impersonal objectivity is likely to make people desire more privacy in their lives. Thoughts and feelings will not be shared for fear of being judged by 'objective' standards; this is, arguably, a modern, western characteristic. Individuals live their lives quite separate from any community, keeping their private thoughts to themselves and criticizing the frailties and weaknesses of others. Their own thoughts, fears, hopes and desires are suppressed in favour of taking up a position of observation, and their minds adopt a state of detachment. The social scientist Theodore Roszak refers to the translation of the scientific notion of objectivity into human affairs as the 'distinctive psychic disease of our age'.

> There is a way to feel and behave objectively, even if one cannot know objectively. Indeed, the capacity of people to depersonalize their conduct – and to do so in good conscience, even with pride – is the distinctive psychic disease of our age.[79]

The importance of objectivity as a universal precondition for all types of knowledge, whether scientific or otherwise, is impressed deeply on the psychology of the modern mind. The behaviourist names it explicitly as a goal of his or her research, while others attempt to adopt 'scientific' objectivity as an ethic, and for yet others it is an unconscious guide to everyday living.

The psychology of the behaviourist seems to rely on the notion that the degree of objectivity in science is directly proportional to the distance one puts between oneself (the subject) and the object of one's study. The dangers of 'anthropomorphic subjectivism' are emphasized; Clark Hull, an American behaviourist, recommended the following as a guard against falling prey to its 'seductions':

> One aid to the attainment of behavioral objectivity is to think in terms of the behavior of subhuman organisms, such as chimpanzees, monkeys, dogs, cats, and albino rats. Unfortunately this form of prophylaxis against subjectivism all too often breaks down when the theorist begins thinking what he would do if he were a rat, a cat, or a chimpanzee. . . . A device much employed by the author has proved itself to be a far more effective prophylaxis. This is to regard, from time to time, the behaving organism

as a completely self-maintaining robot, constructed of
materials as unlike ourselves as may be.[80]

Here, it is all too easy for the behaviourist to forget that he or
she shares qualities with the 'behaving organism'. To be
consistent, the behaviourist should view his or her own
behaviour in terms of say an albino rat, dog, or, as strongly
recommended in the above passage, a 'completely self-
maintaining robot'. Why not take the behavioural point of view
to its natural conclusion, and present it as the observations of
one albino rat about other albino rats? How many behavioural
scientists have the epistemological integrity to compare the
results of their own innovative researches to the stimulated
responses of albino rats? Very few, but then how many albino
rats have epistemological integrity?

The limitations of behaviourism both as a philosophy and a
science are numerous and well documented, so there is no need for
a full discussion of the subject here. The purpose of referring to a
few of behaviourism's inconsistencies in the present context is
simply to illustrate some of the still unresolved problems that lie
behind the modern world-view. Behaviourism suffers from the
same problems as Hume's empirical philosophy in that it cannot
provide any plausible explanation of self-knowledge and can never
achieve objectivity about introspection.

If one takes observable human behaviour as the only criterion
for knowledge of human nature, then it is puzzling that there
appears to be an infinite number of possible observable traits
corresponding to what is experienced as a single mental quality.
Take, for example, anger; it would seem there is an infinite number
of recognizable ways to express it. So mere observation seems to be
an inadequate guide to the state of being angry – and it will be so
for many other states of mind that are obvious when the
metaphysical notion of a mind is allowed for, but seem
incomprehensible in strict empirical terms. The simple act of
observing someone's behaviour is surely not enough to arrive
objectively at adequate knowledge of a human being's mental
state. Yet this assumption is central to an empirically dominated
view of human nature.

The behaviourists' rejection of free will as essential to a scientific description of human behaviour also highlights the many inconsistencies of a purely empirical method of scientific investigation. What would happen if the behaviourist were to accept the implications of rejecting the existence of free will in his or her own case? For one thing, this would mean accepting that the scientific research of the behaviourist is not original, and merely reflects the behaviourist's response to external stimuli. But Skinner's denial of free will is more general than this. He states that the rejection of this concept is central to a scientific description of human nature. On this basis, we would have to conclude that any such 'science' is not science at all, but by its own premiss is the outcome of some mechanical process in which the scientist played no creative part.

We could describe a scientist who holds to this notion of the scientific method as no more than a clerk recording someone else's results. It is well known that people usually consider it an insult if someone suggests that they are not acting with free will; that their actions are outcomes that can be predicted. Tell them that they are quite predictable, and very quickly one will lose friends. Yet, according to the behaviourist, objectivity of this kind is an indispensable method of arriving at a scientific description of human behaviour.

The psychologist Maslow noted the contradiction in the behaviourist's position in not taking account of all behaviour patterns in their research. One neglected factor was how offensive the subject under observation may find the goal of predictability. He wrote:

> When I can predict what a person will do, somehow he feels that it implies a lack of respect for him . . . as if he were no more than a thing. He tends to feel dominated, controlled, outwitted. I have observed instances of a person deliberately upsetting the predictions simply to reaffirm his unpredictability and therefore autonomy and self-governance.[81]

Maslow is stating here what we all know to be true. Our free will is inextricably related to our self-esteem and our self-identity. It is not something we would want to lose. Freedom is something that people are prepared to fight for, suffer for, and die for. In fact, maintaining our own identity, our freedom of choice, and our freedom of expression, is identified with a particularly modern outlook. The 'Declaration of the Rights of Man and of Citizens', which followed the French Revolution in 1789, includes the following passage:

> The National Assembly doth recognise and declare in the presence of the Supreme Being, and with the hope of his blessing and favour, the following sacred rights of men and of citizens: 1. Men are born, and always continue, free and equal in respect of their rights; 2. The end of all political associations is the preservation of the natural and imprescriptible rights of man; and these are Liberty, Property, Security, and Resistance of Oppression.[82]

This declaration of human rights, as advocates of democracy never tire of repeating, is a charter for the modern world-view. It grew out of a revolt against a society in which the will of the people was repressed. It is a charter of freedom and a statement directed against any institution or political system that represses the freedom of the individual.

The modern era is characterized by its liberation from past restraints, whether they be based on religion, class, race, or sex. These rights to self-expression are positive modern developments, since we are no longer forced to follow a certain ideology or religious creed simply because we were born at a certain place or to a certain family. We have much more freedom in social and religious matters than at any other time in human history, and these rights are quite properly regarded as significant modern triumphs. Never has our ability to choose, whether it be on the intellectual, moral or social level, been given such widespread recognition. To act freely, developing one's conscience, according to one's creative impulses and one's sense of oneself, is recognized as the most important of all ways to express our humanity. This is a principle upon which modern society could be said to be founded.

And yet, it diametrically opposes another strand of modern thought, which submits itself to the findings and methods of empirical science. According to empiricists like the behaviourists, free will must be rejected on the authority of science. This is a contradiction in the modern mind that cannot easily be glossed over. On the one hand, free will is a fact of our experience; on the other, its rejection is said to be vital to the scientific study of human nature. On the one hand we have rebelled against social and religious constraints; on the other, we are willing to be prisoners of empirical ideology. This inconsistency lies at the root of much of the spiritual confusion of modern life. It numbs our responses to the many moral challenges of the late twentieth century. Alfred Whitehead noted this underlying contradiction in 1926, when he wrote:

> A scientific realism, based on mechanism, is conjoined with an unwavering belief in the world of men and of the higher animals as being composed of self-determining organisms. This radical inconsistency at the basis of modern thought accounts for much that is half-hearted and wavering in our civilisation. It would be going too far to say that it distracts thought. It enfeebles it, by reason of the inconsistency lurking in the background . . . For instance, the enterprises produced by the individualistic energy of the European peoples presupposes physical actions directed to final causes. But the science which is employed in their development is based on a philosophy which asserts that physical causation is supreme, and which disjoins the physical cause from the final end. It is not popular to dwell on the absolute contradiction here involved. It is a fact, however you gloss it over with phrases.[83]

Whitehead here identifies the heart of the paradox. A mechanically minded science, which only accepts 'brute facts' as scientific, which denies any rationale or purpose or free will behind empirical observations, is in complete contradiction to the freedom of the individual won and insisted upon in modern times in the social and cultural domain. This inconsistency is a good example of the gap between scientific theory and human experience in the modern mind. Behaviourism, to be sure, is a relic of the past, but its underlying positivism and empiricism still lurk in the shadows of modern thought.

5. The Robotomorphic Portrait

Much the same type of empiricism that characterized the behavioural model of human nature is found in the robotomorphic model of man, a self-portrait that has gained considerable popularity in recent years. Ever since the rapid rise of computers from the middle of this century, they have proved extraordinarily successful in performing many tasks formerly done by people. Computers have been central to the modern technological revolution, affecting virtually every sector of society; the changes they have brought about have been fundamental. Computers have now become household items, and their development is still continuing at an unimaginably rapid pace. No human mind, or so it seems, can keep pace with all the latest computer innovations. Computers have proved themselves in many instances not only to be more dependable than human beings, but also more efficient and productive. In short, they are increasingly making people redundant.

It is, no doubt, because of such successes that some people have postulated the human mind is like the software of a computer, and the brain comparable to the hardware. Human behaviour is thus modelled in terms of a set of hierarchical computer programs constantly adapting to the environment. This human self-image sees a person as nothing but a robot, with his or her behaviour in some way preprogrammed – albeit adaptively to the environment. It is emphasized by advocates of this view, who work for the most part in the field of artificial intelligence, that it is quite unimportant whether the basic elements of the computer-mind are composed of biological materials such as neurons, or synthetic materials such as transistors on a silicon chip – the software is independent of the precise material of the hardware with which it works. The topological structure of the interacting components of the hardware is thought to determine the kind of software on which the computer-mind runs. The operations of the mind are modelled on the formal process of symbol-manipulation that occurs in computer programs, where data-storage is represented by on/off states in memory cells, and where data-flow is a series of simple operations of addition and subtraction between banks of memory cells.

It is claimed by some workers in the field of artificial intelligence that computers can 'think', 'feel', have 'desires', 'intentions' and 'ambitions', and 'create' as human beings do. This view, now known as strong AI, holds that even the most rudimentary computational operations can be said to have mental qualities. It has been claimed, for instance, that the operation of a thermostat corresponds to holding 'beliefs'. 'My thermostat has three beliefs,' it has been said. 'It's too hot in here, it's too cold in here, and it's just right in here.'[84]

Mental states, according to the advocates of strong AI, are entailed in the logical functioning of any computer device. To 'think' is equated with the execution of a well-defined sequence of operations. Thoughts are reduced to computer algorithms. Similar to the behavioural model of human nature, the strong AI view is tantamount to a denial of the existence of mental attributes, such as consciousness or will, as experienced by most human beings. Self-identity, self-awareness and the autonomy of free will are regarded, ultimately, as illusory.

The claims of strong AI are very optimistic for the next generation of computers, and remind one of the similar utopian predictions made for behaviourism or positivism. It was claimed a few decades ago that very soon computer-minds would not only be capable of 'thinking', or be 'conscious', but would become so intelligent that we will be 'lucky if they are willing to keep us around as household pets'.[85] Many people have indulged in speculation about computers themselves creating even more 'intelligent' computers, and a future robot utopia where society is ruled by the 'wisdom' of robots: robots solving the world's problems and bringing about world peace. Enthusiasts of strong AI not only state that human nature can be completely explained in terms of the logical operations of a computer, but claim that future computer developments will completely surpass human nature.

All these predictions have failed to come true within the time-scale forecast for them, and it is tempting to take a slightly cynical view and suggest that perhaps they might be better understood in terms of winning higher research grants rather than in any genuine developments in computer research. It is obviously impossible to predict what developments may occur in the future, but while great advances in computer research may be anticipated, it should also be remembered that since the dawn of modern science many models of the mind have been suggested. The mind has been successively likened to a windmill, an engine, a hydraulic system and a telephone exchange, to name but a few. Although the computer-mind model may at present seem very impressive, might it not with the passage of time begin to appear like these past models of the mind, a naive period-piece of technological speculation? Taking a broader historical view of the situation, it seems that every new generation tends to over-estimate the power of its own technological innovations to solve fundamental cosmological mysteries. The development of windmills, engines, hydraulic systems and telephone exchanges was impressive, yet in terms of providing the definitive model for understanding the mind, they now seem quaintly inadequate. Might not computer models of the mind share the same fate?

Like behaviourists before them, advocates of the strong AI approach have their opponents. A dialogue between those who favour the computer-mind model of human nature and those who have raised objections against it involves the same type of discussions that arose in relation to behaviourist claims. Some have objected that a computer-mind is nothing but a formal process of symbol manipulation, which by itself does not have the capability of assigning meaning. Computer programs consist of instructional symbols that turn a series of switches on and off, in much the same way as the rules of grammar in a natural language regulate sentence structure. The computer program, it is pointed out, is no more capable of generating meaning out of its set of instructions than grammatical rules are capable of deriving the meaning of a sentence. There is simply nothing in a set of symbols that contains meaning. A computer's program contains syntax-type information, and not semantic content – and no amount of syntax can produce the semantic content of a language. Likewise, it is argued that no amount of symbol shuffling can duplicate human intentions or purposes; even the symbols themselves have no meaning until we as human beings give them their meaning. Without human participation, the sequence of logical operations of a computer are nothing but a set of switches alternating between their on and off states. The reduction of mental entities to logical strings of symbol manipulation is likened to the reduction of human nature to a series of 'observations' in behaviourism. Both filter out the really important characteristics associated with human minds – such as their capacity to derive meaning.

Many of the discussions about the validity of the computer-mind model for human nature revolve around thought experiments. Assume a computer was devised that could in principle duplicate human behaviour; could we then conclude that the computer can 'think', 'feel', be 'conscious'? Questions in the Turin test were designed to illustrate that such a computer would be indistinguishable from the mind of a human being.[86] But the same problems arise for advocates of strong AI that arose for behaviourists. How does one, for instance, explain self-knowledge? Is self-knowledge the awareness of one's own computational processes as they are occurring? If so, which background algorithms are being executed to produce awareness of these foreground computational processes? Which algorithms in turn allow one to examine these background algorithms? And so on down an infinite chain that does little to capture the experience of self-knowledge, self-awareness or self-identity. It might be replied that there is a root computational process in each human being, which an individual human being can never know consciously; perhaps an electrical pathway that has been written into us by the process of evolution and gives humans the capability to self-reflect. Perhaps, but this captures very little of the experience of freedom in self-discovery with which we are all familiar. Our self-knowledge is punctuated by desires, intentions and purposes for which no amount of background symbol-shuffling can seem to account.

The idea that human nature is fixed to a background computer algorithm denies any autonomy of human thoughts and actions; it denies free will. If one could decipher the root algorithm of human nature, one should be able to predict the behaviour of any human being. But this prediction could simply be invalidated by the individual for whom the prediction is made: upon learning of the prediction, he or she can freely choose to do the opposite. It is not clear how one could program the same degree of autonomy into a robot. All the inconsistencies associated with the behaviourists' rejection of free will also apply to the robotomorphic model. The robotomorphic view of human beings would lead us to conclude that the scientific theories of the supporters of strong AI are the result of nothing but symbol-manipulation, like the enumeration of a set of grammatical rules – 'theories' derived from such a process are not generally considered significant in the scientific field. Much as those who support the strong AI view might be impressed with the power of computer operations, it is difficult to believe that they would be perfectly happy to assign their own actions and thoughts to computer-like operations, which perform a sequence of logical deductions similar to the process of finding an entry in a telephone book. In the field of scientific investigation, such mechanical operations will not produce significant results or add anything to pre-existing knowledge. The robotomorphic model of human nature cannot give a very convincing account of itself.

It is clear that other theories involving the dismissal of mental entities will also lead to internal contradictions. For example, to say that all 'beliefs are illusions' will lead one to conclude that this belief itself, namely the belief that 'all beliefs are illusions', must also be an illusion. Or if one understands one's beliefs to be comparable to the states of a thermostat, then one must accept that this belief itself is also similar to a thermostat's condition, and hence not capable of asserting any profound truth about human nature or the world.

Obviously, the ability of a robot to duplicate the behaviour of a human being does not help us to an understanding of human minds. As is well known, two people can perform exactly the same action for completely different reasons, and it is possible to duplicate someone's actions mechanically without any understanding of their rationale.

For example, there is a great deal of difference between someone who supplies the correct answers in an examination by understanding the questions, and someone who copies the answers of another candidate. The two answers may be identical, but the process of producing each answer is completely different. One is mechanical, and the other comes from understanding the body of knowledge to which the questions refer. One is rewarded, while the other is punished. The difference between these two methods of answering, one the outcome of mental reasoning and thought, the other a mechanical act of copying, characterizes the differences between a human being and a computer.

A computer can perform a very large number of symbol-manipulations in a very short time, but it does so mechanically, in a pre-specified logical sequence. No 'understanding' is required. The answers, as it were, are contained in the program, which is supplied by a human being, and the results follow mechanically from the program instructions. The results of the computer's operations are, to use a logical positivist expression, nothing but tautologies related to the initial axioms contained in the computer program. The computer excels human beings in the speed with which it performs symbol shuffling, but does not devise significant questions. Computers operate with the type of mathematics described by the logical positivists – a tautological sequence of logical operations – but not with mathematics as conceived of by mathematicians.

The debate about whether computers can 'think' involves much more complicated issues than the ones just outlined. Advocates of strong AI usually base their arguments on more sophisticated computers such as parallel computer networks, neural networks, connectionist nets and so on.[87, 88] But many of the same objections apply. A parallel computer might be more adaptive than a sequential computer, in that it is designed to interact with its environment in a certain way, but it will do so according to human-supplied directives. The meaning content in the work of such computers is still supplied by human beings.[89] The computer algorithms employed in either sequential or parallel computers still operate in terms of rules and explicit procedures, and this does little to capture the type of human mathematical reasoning that gave rise to them in the first place, let alone any other human mental activity.[90]

The debate on the robotomorphic view of human beings reflects a clash between an empirical approach to human nature and one that acknowledges the reality of the everyday experience of human autonomy, introspection, self-awareness and self-identity. The empirical approach picks out observable and measurable characteristics of human nature, but as we all know, the workings of the mind are for each one of us a fundamentally private experience. The experience of one's consciousness is not something that can easily be shared with others; the communication channel of our own thoughts is not one that others can tap into (at least, not yet!), but an inner and fundamentally subjective one.

Let us use an analogy. No amount of observation from outside a church will reveal the full colours and intricate patterns of its stained-glass windows. As long as one takes an exterior perspective, one will only see pale reflections of the images to be seen within. Likewise, the richness of mental qualities, their immediacy, their uniqueness, their purpose and meaning, all tell a story that can never be captured by external observation alone.

The inner sanctuary of the mind, the citadel of the soul, is reduced under a purely empiricist gaze to a mere rubble of sense-perceptions. Most modern descriptions of the mind seem to entail this kind of reduction, and are in one way or another a natural consequence of giving priority to empirical observation. The preference for an external approach to describe what every human being experiences as internal and subjective is characteristic of the modern, impersonal world-view.

6. The Survival Machine

Those who describe the development of the modern, scientific world-view in terms of its battle with traditional religion often point to the nineteenth century as a decisive period during which many important victories were won. Although in the seventeenth and eighteenth centuries the authority of the Church was progressively questioned, it was not until the nineteenth that the fundamental principles of religion were openly challenged. A scientific theory that is often cited as having played an important role in all these challenges to religion is Darwin's theory of evolution. This biological theory was variously interpreted, and still is today, as having solved fundamental human mysteries. Darwin's theory has profoundly influenced the modern approach to many problems, ranging from those found in psychology, economics and sociology to the ultimate questions of our existence. In particular, many who have questioned basic religious principles in the modern era, such as the existence of God, did so, and still do, on the authority of the theory of evolution.

With hindsight, many of the ideological arguments using Darwin's theory now seem naive. The social Darwinians, for example, are now generally recognized to have manipulated Darwinian theory for their own philosophical ends. Herbert Spencer, who used Darwin's theory to justify a ruthless style of capitalism, is today largely discredited.[91] Marx also put Darwin's theory to ideological use, stating it to be a model for economic change, and claiming that his own theory of social and economic change was 'scientific'.

The importance of Darwin's theory in the questioning of

fundamental religious beliefs can be exaggerated. Naturally, influential people had publicly questioned the existence of God long before the publication of Darwin's theory, such as the philosopher and ex-theologian turned atheist Ludwig Feuerbach, who developed much of his philosophy in the early part of the nineteenth century.

Feuerbach influenced the thinking of many later atheists. He captured the intellectually rebellious mood of the nineteenth century against religion by writing that he was living in a 'period of the decline of Christianity'[92] and that the golden age of Christianity had long since passed. He also articulated contemporary thought when he stated that his thinking had progressed through the stages of belief in first God, then in reason, then in man. He wrote: 'God was my first thought, reason my second, man my third and last thought'.[93] Feuerbach reversed the earlier notion that humanity was a thought in God's mind, and described God as a mere belief-thought in human minds. Feuerbach concluded that God was a mere 'projection of man', and had no objective existence, only a psychological one.

Feuerbach's philosophy had enduring impact, mainly psychological. For the later intellectuals who are commonly cited as having a profound role in shaping the modern mind, God was a fictitious product of the human mind. Freud, for instance, said the idea of God originated in the need to have a father figure for adults. Marx added social dimensions to a similar theme when he described religion as an 'opiate of the people'. Nietzsche, who stated that 'God is dead' and sought to replace meek religious values with ones founded on the human 'will to power', continued a line of reasoning that was already well established. As in the case of Feuerbach's philosophy, these movements towards secularism were inextricably linked to a revolt against the corruption of Christianity. This century, the trend towards scientific rationalism and existential humanism has steadily continued, with both presenting themselves as alternative philosophies to religion, and becoming, in effect, surrogate religions.

The theory of evolution has a distinctive place in the ideological struggle to replace the traditional religious world-view with a scientific and humanist one. It is often put forward as the modern creation myth, in place of the traditional biblical one, and presented as the secular explanation of our origins, vying with religion for our hearts and minds. The philosopher Mary Midgley has referred to the theory of evolution as the 'religion of evolution', and she writes:

> Evolution is the creation-myth of our age. By telling us our origins it shapes our views of what we are. It influences not just our thought, but our feelings and actions too, in a way which goes far beyond its official function as a biological theory.[94]

Although it is claimed that the theory has solved the ultimate mysteries of human existence, it is doubtful whether such a solution can be provided by a limited scientific theory, which can always be improved upon, and even possibly disproved. In any case, the theory of evolution as understood by some of its more enthusiastic devotees bears remarkable similarities to the religious dogmas it seeks to replace. The absolute nature of some claims lead one to conclude that the theory of evolution is, for some, a quasi-religious belief. Consider, for example, the statement of the Nobel prize-winning biologist Jacques Monod, who wrote:

> Chance alone is the source of every innovation, of all the biosphere. Pure chance, absolutely free but blind, at the root of the stupendous edifice of evolution: this concept of modern biology is no longer one among other possible or even conceivable hypotheses. It is today the sole conceivable hypothesis . . . and nothing warrants the supposition (or the hope) that conceptions about this should, or ever could, be revised.[95]

The same quasi-religious devotion to the theory of evolution is expressed by the zoologist Richard Dawkins who, in his book *The Blind Watchmaker*, sets out to convince the reader that the theory of evolution has solved once and for all the great cosmological mystery of our origins. Dawkins writes:

This book is written in the conviction that our own existence once presented the greatest of all mysteries, but that it is a mystery no longer because it is solved. Darwin and Wallace solved it, though we shall continue to add footnotes to their solution for a while yet . . . I want to persuade the reader, not just that the Darwinian world-view happens to be true, but that it is the only known theory that could, in principle, solve the mystery of our existence.[96]

Both these passages remind one of a profession of faith; they urge the faithful to follow the one true path of evolutionary theory, while denouncing other beliefs to be false. It should be recognized that this kind of quasi-religious conviction about Darwin's theory is only articulated by a small minority. Yet its basic beliefs are implicitly shared by the majority of people in western intellectual circles. Such attitudes make it difficult to appreciate the genuine scientific merit of Darwin's theory, and create an atmosphere in which different theories of human nature compete with one another on irreconcilable ideological grounds.

Darwin's theory of natural selection can be summarized as a struggle for existence; individual creatures compete for limited food and other resources, and only those best adapted to the environment survive, thus leaving the most descendants. Variations in the genetic make-up of individual creatures, according to the theory, occur spontaneously in the form of genetic mutations, and the traits that gradually emerge will be those best adapted to survival in the relevant environment. In this way, a species could change its nature and evolve into another species; all species are speculated to have arisen from the same origin, pushed in their different directions by the same mechanism under different environmental circumstances.

This process is called 'natural' selection in order to distinguish it from artificial methods of selection for plants and animals. Darwin wrote:

Owing to this struggle for life, any variation, however slight, and from whatever cause preceding, if it be any

degree profitable to an individual of any species . . . will
tend to the preservation of that individual, and will
generally be inherited by its offspring.[97]

Understanding of genes and the mechanisms of inheritance only
developed after the publication of Darwin's theory, with the work
of Gregor Mendel early this century. Most scientists would agree
that life on earth, including human life, has evolved, but disputes
arise about the precise nature of the mechanisms involved, and
whether they can all be reduced to a simple one, like natural
selection. Controversies also occur over the philosophical
implications of the theory.

Immediately after its publication, Darwin's theory was used to
devalue the nature of humanity. If we shared a common ancestry
with animals, did this not tend to destroy any claims for our
uniqueness, theological or otherwise? Humanity, instead of being
made in the image of God, was seen as a creature moulded out of
survival pressures, which were no more designed with a special
purpose than the direction of the wind is pre-determined.

It is easy to understand how Darwin's theory could be
interpreted as having brought about a Copernican revolution in
the hierarchy of terrestrial creatures: humanity appeared to lose its
centrality in the universe of living things, and was consigned to an
orbit, along with all other creatures, around the mechanism of
natural selection. This paradigm shift underlies most modern
descriptions of human nature. One can trace its influence on the
psychology of Freud, who regarded his own work as continuing the
trend in which he understood Darwin's work to have had an
important role. Freud further developed the theme by postulating
that human nature was dominated by subconscious instinctual
drives, which impaired the operation of the rational faculty. So,
what was previously regarded as a divine attribute, human reason,
unique to humanity and a reflection of God, was described as
merely a slave to instinctual drives.

Freud's ideas have had profound influence on theories of
human nature this century. Many similar theories, also modelling
human nature in terms of animal behaviour, took the theory of
evolution as their authority for denying the uniqueness of human

nature. The typical starting point for such theories is to assume that animal behaviour can provide a sufficient guide for understanding human behaviour, as with the behaviourists and their assumption that human behaviour could be adequately described by studying the behaviour of albino rats.

In the 1960s and early 1970s, the notion that human behaviour was to be understood in terms of primordial biological instincts was popularized by many writers, such as the ethologist Konrad Lorenz and the writer Desmond Morris.[98,99] All kinds of human disputes and the hierarchical divisions in society were compared with the territorial and other conflicts of animals. Human aggression, in particular, was described as rooted in in-built biological pressures, whose release was essentially uncontrollable and spontaneous. A wide range of aggressive behaviour, including war, crime, forms of vandalism, and sadism, were cited as examples of instinctual pressures surfacing in human behaviour. Also, theories generalized from the violent behaviour of animals kept in captivity were used to explain the nature of urban violence among humans. People living in crowded conditions in cities were compared to animals caged in zoos.[100]

The conclusions of those who formulated animal instinctivist models of human nature have generally been pessimistic about the prospect of eliminating war. Freud, Lorenz, Morris and others have expressed doubts, based on supposedly inherent biological constraints, that humanity will ever be able to live peacefully. Such conclusions have an important moral consequence. Since animal instinctivist models have come to dominate popular conceptions of human nature, they tend to blunt efforts to establish world peace. This model of human nature gives 'scientific' support to the widespread belief that warfare is caused by an incorrigibly selfish strand in human nature. Efforts towards attaining world peace are dismissed as utopian and unrealistic, because of an underlying belief that animal instincts dominate human behaviour.

Much of the inspiration for animal instinctivist models comes directly from the theory of evolution. Lorenz, for example, declares: 'I believe in the power of human reason, as I believe in the power of natural selection.'[101] It is uttered like a manifesto for social change, and indeed that is the context in which Lorenz stated it. He goes on to describe, in directly religious terms, how he believes natural selection will soon generate new 'commandments': 'I believe that this, in the not too distant future, will endow our descendants with the faculty of fulfilling the greatest and most beautiful of all commandments.'[102] Similar articles of faith, although less explicit, are involved in taking natural selection as the key principle for understanding social behaviour, human nature and our collective future. The pre-eminent position given to the theory of evolution is revealing of the psychology of our age.

There are obvious problems in generalizing natural selection into a 'theory of everything'. Natural selection describes a mechanism that operates primarily on the individual level and governs the successful inheritance of genetic traits. It will thus automatically filter out human social phenomena, such as morality. How can natural selection account for altruism, and in particular unselfish acts towards genetically unrelated people? If morality must also be a genetically inherited trait, where is the genetic advantage in altruistic acts that involve generosity to someone who cannot propagate one's genes? If our actions are to be explained in terms of preserving the human gene pool as a whole, where does the ethic of being kind to animals come from? The ethic of altruism is only part of a wider moral outlook, which stresses the importance for humanity of being in harmony with all forms of life. If preserving our human gene pool is so important, what motivates those people who work to protect endangered species? If individuals were merely 'survival machines' enabling genes to flourish and multiply, as suggested by Richard Dawkins, why do human beings perform acts of altruism, labour for justice, suffer for principles of truth, create art, and so on, as everyone knows they do? How does one explain the widespread practice of celibacy in terms of maximizing genetic inheritance? How is it genetically advantageous for the prisoner of conscience to spend his or her whole life in prison to defend the principle of individual freedom of expression or religious practice? Surely such actions are more understandable in terms of human education and culture, rather than in terms of genetic propagation. In sum, genetic reductionism cannot provide a convincing account of human morality.

Describing all human behaviour as a reaction to survival pressures leads to many possible abuses. It can be used to give 'scientific' credence to inhumane ideologies; for example, supporting amoral exploitation of the less 'successful' classes or persecution of 'inferior' races. Genetic reductionism, when blindly applied to human behaviour, can also lead one to condone extreme forms of individualism and selfishness. The theory of evolution as a quasi-religious belief leads to an ethic of self-interest, which is undeniably the ethic of modern western societies. Mary Midgley writes:

> Social Darwinism or Spencerism is the unofficial religion of the West. The official western religion, Christianity, is well known to be rather demanding and to have its eye on the next world rather than this one. In such situations, other doctrines step in to fill the gap. People want a religion for this world as well. They find it in the worship of individual success . . . and it is widely believed that the theory of evolution proves this kind of narrowly self-assertive motivation to be not just an unfortunate response to certain local social conditions, but fundamental, universal and in some sense the law of life.[103]

Evolutionary theory can be tacitly used by all those intent on justifying ruthless competition, on making individual success their ultimate goal in life, and on putting their self-interest before the welfare of others. Biological theory can become a philosophical prop to egoism, and a way of avoiding moral commitment.

The simple theory that survival pressures mould human behaviour can provide no explanation for one very important sphere of human activity: scientific investigation. Here, a quasi-religious belief in natural selection is not compatible with a belief in human reason. How is scientific investigation to be explained solely in terms of successful genetic inheritance? Is science merely another vehicle by which selfish genes can propagate? Here one is forced to recognize an important philosophical fallacy in all the uncritical uses of natural selection as a model of human behaviour: the framers of such generalizations will be robbed of their own rationality. This self-defeat awaits all those who seek to reduce human nature to its animal counterpart. Were Freud's so-called scientific theories not weakened if he himself was ruled by subconscious animal drives? Was Freud, in fact, one of the few people in modern times who succeeded in making their individual neurosis a universal one? His belief in human rationality, and in particular the rationality of his own scientific work, is undermined by the conclusions of this very same work.

Scepticism about human reason is inherently self-defeating. The same conclusion might be drawn about Lorenz when we see that his belief in the power of human reason is coupled with a conviction that the mechanism of natural selection determines all human behaviour. The two beliefs are incompatible. There is nothing in survival pressures which accounts for human reason, and Lorenz believes that the principle of natural selection is all-encompassing, not just one factor among many others in our evolution, which is how many other biologists understand it. The inconsistency comes from understanding natural selection to be a theory that can explain everything.

There are formidable philosophical problems involved in attempting to make the principle of natural selection fully descriptive of human minds and culture. This principle is of course useful in understanding some aspects of human nature, such as our 'natural' sympathies and aversions, which indeed may derive from survival pressures. But fundamental philosophical problems occur when this is extrapolated into the founding principle upon which all human nature is to be understood. The reasons for making it such an all-encompassing theory no doubt originate in ideological motives, especially the attempt to promote the theory of evolution as a secular creation myth about human origins that can vie with religious accounts. But the fact that human beings share much in common with animals now, and have done in the past, does not make them equivalent to animals in all respects. We might not be able to *explain* the differences between human beings and animals, but that is no reason for *ignoring* them. Our bodies appear to have more in common with animals than our minds, and there may be important reasons for this difference; perhaps human beings only partially share a common ancestry with animals.

It is interesting to note in this context that Alfred Russel

Wallace, who arrived independently at the theory of natural selection around the same time as Darwin, did not reduce human nature to animal nature. Wallace believed that natural selection provided a plausible account of the development of the human body, but not the characteristics of the human mind. He could not believe that 'spiritual' characteristics could be reduced to a struggle for physical survival, and stressed that human nature could only be understood in terms of such characteristics, which include the 'persevering search of the scientific worker':

> Thus alone can we understand the constancy of the martyr, the unselfishness of the philanthropist, the devotion of the patriot, the enthusiasm of the artist and the resolute and persevering search of the scientific worker after nature's secrets. Thus we may perceive that the love of truth, the delight in beauty, the passion for justice, and the thrill of exultation with which we hear of any act of courageous self-sacrifice, are the workings within us of a higher nature which has not been developed by means of the struggle for material existence.[104]

It is clear that while the mechanism of natural selection may have played an important part in human evolution, one cannot insist that it provides all the answers about human existence. Human beings might have been a species apart from other animals right from the beginning of the evolutionary process.

If one compares a new-born human baby with a baby chimpanzee, the two will for a significant period appear quite alike – in purely physical terms. It is only after they reach a stage well into infancy that one will start to observe significant behavioural differences between them. If one only assesses them in terms of bodily similarity, one will be blind to their obvious mental differences; the same error might be said to be involved in concluding that because human beings and animals are thought to derive from the same ancestry – a conjecture based on physical observations – they are also identical in mental terms. This is like concluding that the physical similarity between two different seeds is reason enough to expect them to bear the same type of fruit when they are planted in the ground. Only with time does one discover the differences that may be latent within the seeds. Natural selection pressures might have acted on the human race and animal alike, but this cannot lead one to conclude that there is no fundamental difference between them.

The naive notion that the theory of evolution has somehow disproved the existence of God is widespread today, and it is completely false. The notion rests on at least two assumptions. The first is that the theory of evolution provides a 'theory of everything'. The second relies on a belief that nature's mechanisms are essentially blind; that they function independently of meanings and purposes. This is clearly a philosophical bias – a modern prejudice; there is no philosophical or scientific reason why the laws of nature should function separately from religious purposes.

If the phenomenon of evolution is ultimately dependent on the laws of physics, for example, where do the laws of physics come from? How do we know that there is not a cosmic design behind the laws of physics? It may be that the laws of physics were 'designed' to create the conditions in which life would evolve. Indeed some physicists and astronomers have recently suggested exactly this: that the evolution of life and our own existence seem to have been critically dependent on the values of certain universal constants in nature which, if differing even marginally from their present values, would have precluded the conditions necessary for life on earth. Astronomer John Barrow and physicist Frank Tipler, in their book *The Anthropic Cosmological Principle*,[105] suggest that there is reason enough to be open to the idea of 'design' in the universe. Not all scientists draw anti-religious conclusions from the theory of evolution; in fact, the philosophy of the theologian and scientist Pierre Teilhard de Chardin is founded on generalizing Darwin's theory of evolution as a universal religious archetype.

The widespread belief that human aggression derives from an uncontrollable biological urge to act on innate instincts is also unsupported by scientific research. The pessimistic conclusions of Freud, Lorenz and Morris about the possibility of achieving a peaceful world, although receiving considerable popular attention, are largely unfounded. The psychologist Erich Fromm, in his book

The Anatomy of Human Destructiveness, presents evidence from the fields of neurophysiology, animal behaviour, palaeontology and anthropology to show that human aggression cannot simply be modelled in terms of animal aggression. Fromm points out that human beings were not predatory hunters in the past, but were largely vegetarian. It is easy to exaggerate the importance of aggression in the behaviour of animals; the ability to co-operate is just as likely to improve the chances of survival as the ability to fight. Fromm writes that if all human beings shared the instincts of chimpanzees (our nearest genetic neighbours), 'then we would have a much more peaceful world'.[106] Fromm also argues that human aggression is much more complex than animal aggression, and simple analogies based on animal behaviour mask these additional factors.

He distinguishes two types of aggression in humans. The first he refers to as 'benign aggression', which human beings do indeed share with animals. This type of aggression is largely defensive, and is used in ensuring the survival of the individual and the species. It can be greatly reduced by minimizing danger factors, and humanitarian and religious values, with their ideals of universal brotherhood and co-operation, play an important role in eliminating this type of aggression. The second type Fromm calls 'malignant aggression', and this he takes to be uniquely human. This type of aggression is manifested in sadism and is caused by the lack of fulfilment of human potential, and the effects of exploitation and manipulation. It is associated with boredom and triviality, and could be greatly reduced by creating a favourable social and cultural environment:

> The malignant forms of aggression . . . are not innate; hence, they can be substantially reduced when the socio-economic conditions are replaced by conditions that are favourable to the full development of man's genuine needs and capacities; to the development of human self-activity and man's creative power as its own end. Exploitation and manipulation produce boredom and triviality; they cripple man, and all factors that make man into a psychic cripple turn him also into a sadist or a destroyer.[107]

Fromm also dispels the notion that urban human aggression can be likened to animal aggression under conditions of captivity, or that overcrowding is responsible for increasing aggression in humans. Human aggression is not rooted in territorial-type intrusions, but arises from a combination of psychological and social factors. Fromm points out that only when crowded conditions are combined with stress and poverty are human beings likely to be aggressive. Otherwise, they not only display remarkable tolerance of one another under crowded conditions, but are capable of developing profound bonds. The comradeship and mutual understanding that can prevail in a kibbutz is cited as an example of people living together happily under crowded conditions. Other examples include the spirit of unity prevailing in a tightly packed air-raid shelter during a bombardment.

Human behaviour, therefore, cannot simply be reduced to its animal equivalent. There are psychological factors in human beings, such as boredom and lack of fulfilment, that are highly conducive to violence. People have goals, ideals, reasons, beliefs and so on that cannot all be reduced to biological instincts. In particular, warfare is a complex, peculiarly human activity that cannot be separated from its underlying aims and values. To discuss the causes of war purely in terms of uncontrollable biological urges is to completely misunderstand the nature of war. Erich Fromm writes:

> The thesis that war is caused by innate human destructiveness is plainly absurd for anyone who has even the slightest knowledge of history. The Babylonians, the Greeks, up to the statesmen of our time, have planned war for what they thought were very realistic reasons and weighed the pros and cons very thoroughly, even though, naturally, their calculations were erroneous. Their motives were manifold: land for cultivation, riches, slaves, raw materials, markets, expansion – and defence.[108]

This brings out the obvious point that warfare is not an uncontrollable biological activity, but requires planning and careful execution. The widespread belief that warfare is rooted in a release of primordial biological instincts, with its accompanying appeal to scientific theory as its authority, is not only misleading but extremely dangerous. The pessimism it creates blunts our collective efforts to achieve peace. In view of the important moral consequences of such misinformation, a team of international scientists met in Seville in May 1986 to issue a 'Statement on Violence'. The statement sets out to dispel pseudo-scientific myths and popular misconceptions about human nature:

> Believing that it is our responsibility to address from our particular disciplines the most dangerous and destructive activities of our species, violence and war; recognising that science is a human cultural product which cannot be definitive or all encompassing . . . we challenge a number of alleged biological findings that have been used, even by some in our disciplines, to justify violence and war . . . misuse of scientific theories and data to justify violence and war is not new but has been made since the advent of modern science. For example, the theory of evolution has been used to justify not only war, but also genocide, colonialism, and suppression of the weak.[109]

The statement goes on to assert that it is scientifically incorrect to say that humanity has inherited a tendency to make war from animal ancestors; or that violent behaviour is programmed genetically into human nature; or that there has been a selection of more aggressive types of behaviour rather than co-operative behaviour in the course of evolution; or that human beings have a 'violent brain'; or that war can be understood in terms of a single biological instinct.

> It is scientifically incorrect to say that we have inherited a tendency to make war from our animal ancestors. Although fighting occurs widely throughout animal species, only a few cases of destructive intra-species fighting between organized groups have ever been reported among naturally living species, and none of these involve the use of tools designed to be weapons. Normal predatory

feeding upon other species cannot be equated with intra-species violence. Warfare is a peculiarly human phenomenon and does not occur in other animals.

The confusion over what science reveals about human nature is characteristic of our time. The reduction of human nature to animal nature is not supported by the findings of any single scientific theory or set of scientific theories; there is no direct scientific link between the two, yet there is undoubtedly a psychological one. In the modern mind, the denial of human uniqueness is associated with adopting a scientific description of human nature. Misapplied scientific theories are all too easily integrated into the wider ideological struggle between a modern secular world-view and traditional religion.

Part Two

··

PERSONAL KNOWLEDGE

7. Selection and Interpretation in Science: the Power of the Mind

The notion that science is primarily dominated by the discovery of impersonal facts masks other equally important characteristics that are well known to scientists themselves. To begin with, an obvious point is that facts do not somehow materialize in the scientist's mind when he or she records observations, but are invariably the result of careful selection. There is a potentially infinite number of observations to be made by a scientist, but only a few are usually relevant to the investigation in hand.

Consider for example Heinrich Hertz's experiment, performed in 1888, that enabled him to produce and detect radio waves for the first time. If he had been completely unbiased (or objective) in his observations, along with registering currents in electrical circuits he should also have noted the colour of his meters, or the colour and size of his shoes. This he did not do. He did not, for instance, record the weather conditions at the time of his experiment, the size of his laboratory, or other details. But the question is, how did Hertz decide which observations to record? How does one decide between an irrelevant observation (or fact) and a significant one? As most scientists know, there is no formal way of doing so.

Separating relevant observations from irrelevant ones involves the scientist in making a judgement, which is based on his or her background knowledge and experience – or preconceptions and biases. There is no general rule for deciding which observations to record, and which ones to discard; it requires an act of judgement that is necessarily personal and subjective. Observations relevant to the experiment do not automatically present themselves to the mind of the scientist.

It is also important to realize that the act of selecting observations is a creative one requiring a skill like that of a craftsman. The sculptor, for instance, shapes his or her formless lump of clay according to a spiritual vision of beauty and harmony, which requires prior experience and knowledge. Likewise, the scientist creatively forms a set of relevant facts, discarding irrelevant ones, constantly 'shaping' them with the purpose of relating them to a specific theory or experiment. The scientist is not objective, and does not record facts without an underlying purpose. On the contrary, a good scientist is characterized by extreme selectiveness and is highly purposeful.

It is interesting to note that one of the observations that appeared irrelevant to Hertz's experiment, namely the size of the room in which he was working, turned out to be highly significant. The velocity of the electromagnetic waves should, according to Maxwell's theory, have been equal to the speed of light, yet Hertz consistently measured a different speed. He was never able to explain why the experimental values should differ from the theoretical ones in this way. It was only later realized that the radio waves emitted from his apparatus were being reflected by the walls of his laboratory and were interfering with his measurements – the size of the room had actually been an important parameter in explaining the results! Yet there was no logical, formal or impersonal method Hertz could have applied in advance of conducting his experiment to help him distinguish the significant observations from the insignificant ones. Hertz used personal, subjective judgements, based on his experience as a scientist to help him choose the data he recorded.

Science, therefore, requires skills that are highly purposeful, selective and creative, and involves the scientist in making judgements that cannot be specified by a set of formal instructions. A passive mind, such as that described by the empiricist's model of human nature, is not the kind that can easily make the judgements demanded of a scientist.

The scientist cannot always choose the same set of

observations. Significant facts can only be selected with reference to the actual experiment to be performed or the theory that is being formulated. This means that a scientist must not be predisposed towards choosing certain types of data for every experiment, even if he or she is inclined to do so out of habit (conditioning), or is neurologically 'programmed' to do so. Whatever the source of a predisposition, whether emotional, social, biological or chemical, the scientist needs to override bias and select data according to intellectual and scientific criteria. Flexibility is necessary, as is autonomy. The scientist must be objective only in this sense: that prior dispositions do not prevent him or her from distinguishing relevant from irrelevant facts. Although the judgements involved are irreducibly subjective, he or she must be allowed to make them freely.

Since facts are not passively recorded in the mind of a scientist but are selected, it follows that they are inherently theory-laden. Another area that highlights the nature of facts in science is their interpretation. Not only are they constantly being selected, they are also constantly interpreted.

After certain observations have been selected from an experiment to test a specific theory, the scientist must decide if the data gathered from the experiment refute the theory, suggest modifications to it, or confirm it? How does one decide on the impact of experimental data on the theory being tested? Again, there is no formal way of deciding how the results of an experiment are to be interpreted. There is no magic formula that one can apply to assess the results. Another act of judgement is required from the scientist, entailing further skill. There is no predefined, universally accepted level of evidence that one can decide either falsifies a theory, proves it, or leaves its status unchanged – this requires subjective decisions that depend on the individual nature of the problem under investigation, and on the personal judgements of the scientist. Facts do not automatically prove a theory to be correct, as a positivist model of science would suggest.

The facts arising from an experiment need to be interpreted in the light of many considerations. The results of an experiment may for instance be faulty; the scientist must be careful not to reject the theory on the basis of faulty observations. There are many examples in science where observations are rejected and the theory is retained. Few scientific theories are directly falsifiable, and in practice, whenever a conflict occurs, whether a theory is to be rejected or the observations are to be discarded is a personal judgement of the scientist involved.

There has been much discussion about whether the falsifiability criterion provides an adequate basis for conducting scientific investigation. Yet Karl Popper, to whom the criterion is attributed, did not present it either as an infallible method of science or as a test of truth in the positivist sense. He did not use it to distinguish between scientific concepts and 'meaningless' concepts. Popper accepted that there was much in the field of scientific investigation that could not be articulated, and only used the falsifiability criterion as a rough demarcation between science and non-science.[110]

The Copernican theory serves as a good example of the limitations of a simple falsifiability criterion in science, and why in practice no scientist ever uses it. Observations made by the naked eye, just after the Copernican theory was formulated, suggested that the shape of the planet Venus was constant, invalidating the Copernican prediction that it should change during the course of the year. Yet the Copernican theory was retained and these observations were not trusted. Later, it was confirmed – with the aid of a telescope – that the size of Venus did change. The original judgement was later confirmed as a good one, but there was no way of formally deciding at the time – no set of logical, impersonal rules to apply – whether the Copernican theory was to be refuted or accepted on the basis of observations of the planet Venus. The fate of the Copernican theory was not automatically decided by the known 'facts'. It requires a free, personal judgement on the part of the scientist, and no amount of rules or procedures can decide how he or she must interpret the evidence.

A single theory very rarely exists in isolation. It invariably forms a part of a wider background theory, which itself may be revised at any stage of the scientific investigation. This point is well put by the philosopher Thomas Kuhn, who states that there is a world-view behind every scientific theory, one that often exists in the form of traditions. Kuhn calls them 'paradigms'. He considers that significant scientific advances are those that lead to the acquisition of new paradigms.[111] These background theories themselves employ a host of auxiliary postulates and it may be that a clash between theory and experimental results arises out of a misunderstanding of an auxiliary postulate. This is quite often the case in science, and a good scientist is always alert to the possibility.

The manner in which the planet Neptune was discovered illustrates this point. It appeared that the orbit of the planet Uranus deviated considerably from the orbit predicted for it by Newtonian physics. In an attempt to interpret these results, Leverrier in France and Adams in England conjectured the existence of another planet, hitherto undetected, accounting for the apparent discrepancy between theory and practice. From this bold speculation, it was possible to predict where such a planet would be located, if of a reasonable size. When Galle pointed a telescope into this patch of the sky, he confirmed the sighting of Neptune.[112] There was no infallible method of deciding whether Newton's theory, experimental observation, or auxiliary postulates were at fault; the possibilities were many. It required a personal judgement, involving speculation (in the sense of going beyond the given observations) to interpret the facts.

There are many possible interpretations one can give to a set of experimental results or observations, yet a good scientist can narrow down these possibilities to a few plausible ones. As with the selection of relevant facts from among irrelevant ones, the scientist must distinguish plausible theories from implausible ones. Only a poor scientist seeks to escape from this type of personal involvement with science. The good scientist seeks to be passionately involved in his or her research.

The discussion about the theory-laden nature of facts has been central to the philosophy of science this century. The philosophies of Popper, Kuhn and Feyerabend, for example, are frequently cited as significant reactions to positivism.[113] In the following pages, however, an aspect of scientific investigation will be described which has as yet received comparatively little attention in the contemporary philosophy of science.

The discussion here draws much from the author's own professional experience as a scientist, and also from the works of the philosopher and scientist Michael Polanyi. Polanyi is a largely unrecognized figure in the mainstream philosophy of science, yet he not only anticipated many of the criticisms of positivism associated with Popper, Kuhn and Feyerabend, but his work in many respects goes beyond theirs. His main theme, that science is founded upon a community of inquirers held together by a common faith in transcendent obligations and beliefs, was first articulated in 1946 in his book *Science, Faith and Society*.[114] In many respects, Polanyi's work is one of the clearest expositions of science as work founded upon personal commitment.

It is important from the outset to emphasize that in bringing out the role of faith, truth and meaning in scientific investigation, the author does not mean to suggest that scientific truths are subjective. These pages are written in the conviction that the ideal of objectivity in science is a good one. It is precisely this, the universality of science, independent of specific cultural beliefs, that gives it its force and power. The history of science is a testimony to its multiculturalism; the international nature of modern science is beyond dispute. The argument is really about what we mean by objectivity. Does it, for instance, as implied by advocates of positivism, have anything to do with suspending beliefs about humanity's significance in the cosmos? Just because science searches for objective truths does not mean that it has a readily identifiable method, or that we can describe it with logical precision. Nor does it mean that no other human pursuits can be described as objective. The task here is to enlarge upon our notion of objectivity, and free it from its positivist connotations.

In selecting and interpreting facts, in constructing plausible theories and choosing between rival ones, the mind of a scientist plays an active role, not a passive one. Without the creative participation of the mind, facts would be little more than a succession of unconnected sensations. The mind selects, interprets and weaves together such sensations into a comprehensible picture of the world and ourselves, it does not operate by translating perceptions into thoughts in a one-to-one correspondence. The character of one's mind is not simply described by the sum of all the input sensations that one has received. Observations are only the beginning of the mental process; they are subsequently translated into something of an entirely different category. As many philosophers from Aristotle to Kant have noted, the mind makes an intuitive leap from a set of 'particulars' to a 'universal'. A finite number of facts are translated into an infinite, inexhaustible entity, a mental category.

To understand the characteristics of a mental category, consider the example of the concept of 'chairs'. From the different examples of chairs that one has observed, finite in number, one is led to the concept of chairs in general: from this or that chair, to chairs as a class. This mental entity is a universal in the sense that it does not relate to any particular chair, that is, there is no correspondence with anything that one can point to in the external world called 'chairs'. This ability of the mind to go from a set of particulars to a universal has been recognized throughout history as the foundation of all knowledge. In particular, Aristotle noted its primary role in scientific investigation. The ability is still as mysterious and as fundamental in relation to science as it was when people of ancient times began to marvel at it. The minds of human beings are constantly switching back and forth between particulars and universals like the action of breathing in and out.

The act of arriving at a universal mental category is essentially a holistic one: no amount of shuffling a set of particulars, and no increase in their numbers, can create a corresponding universal. Moreover, a fundamental characteristic of these universals is that they are inexhaustible, that is, they contain an infinite number of particulars. One can, for instance, continue indefinitely to list different types of chairs, yet never completely specify what is meant by the universal term 'chairs'. The class of all chairs involves a tacit integration of the finite perceptions of different chairs, into an intuitively created entity that somehow embraces all chairs. The mind converts finite sensations into an infinite class, which cannot be reduced to its constituent parts. A universal is therefore irreducible, holistic and intuitive in character, and arriving at one is a creative act that cannot be produced by applying a set of mechanical operations to input sensations.

Some concepts in mathematics aptly illustrate this. Take, for instance, the concept of infinity: at some point in the act of counting one, two, three and so on, there appeared the concept of infinity, a mental entity that embraces all numbers simultaneously and yet, at the same time, is not a number. How is the mind able to leap intuitively to the set of all integers, as embraced by the concept of infinity, from the contemplation of a limited number of integers? This is clearly a process of extrapolation that goes beyond the finite number of input sensations to the brain; infinity is a creative construction of the mind. Something has been added to the sequence of input sensations that was not there before. Where can one point to infinity in the external world? It is not of the same category as a number? The mind is continually transcending the given facts in this way, leaping beyond them to perform creative, intuitive acts of integration.

Even a single number, say the number two, is a universal – an inexhaustible set arrived at by an infinite leap of integration. The number two is grounded in our experience of the world, yet to describe fully what we mean by the number two is not at all easy. An exact definition of any number remains, after thousands of years of science and philosophy, a mystery. This is related to the problem of specifying an infinite class by listing a finite number of its members. We all know intuitively what we mean by a number, yet when it comes to arriving at a watertight definition of it, the task has somehow eluded us.

The concepts of infinity and zero are more complicated than the concept of a number. What can we point to in the external world that gives rise to the concept of zero? It is an imaginative construct of the mind. Infinity and zero are not numbers, as all mathematicians are taught at the very beginning of their study. One cannot subtract infinities, add them, or multiply them, in the same way that one can perform arithmetical operations with numbers. Infinity and zero lie outside the domain of the normal rules of arithmetic. Much confusion is caused if one tries to manipulate infinity or zero like an ordinary number. Anyone who has written a computer program will have experienced a problem of a 'divide by zero' or a 'real number overflow' error at some stage – automatically bringing the program to a halt. Computers are not adept at handling the concept of zero or infinity, and any attempt at treating them like numbers in a computer program will lead to nonsensical results. The two concepts need special procedures, and indeed much of the teaching of mathematics in the foundation courses of universities deals precisely with this issue.

Mathematics is fundamentally concerned with such abstractions. Consider, for example, the square root of −1. The technical reader will recognize this as a concept vitally important to applied mathematics, physics and engineering. The concept has greatly helped in modelling important properties in science, such as the phase relationship between waves, and has great practical significance in science, yet what is it exactly? The square root of −1 is not a number. It contravenes the normal rules of arithmetic, which do not allow for the square root of a negative number. One cannot point to anything in the external world and call it 'the square root of −1'. It is clearly a creative construct of the mind. Although initially founded in sense perceptions, such concepts move immeasurably far beyond them.

Mathematics has a life of its own, and is a world of its own. It uses sense perceptions as raw material, and then creates a world infinitely far removed from them − just as the finished piece of sculpture produced by an artist transcends the initial formless clay from which it was made. Where in nature does one find a perfect circle? Where does one observe the number zero? The abstract concepts of mathematics have been vital to the progress of science, but why should abstract constructs of the mind so powerfully describe nature? If human beings had never existed, would the concept of a circle exist? Could mathematics exist without the power and creativity of human minds? These are mysteries that philosophers and scientists have studied for centuries. Despite all our modern scientific progress, we are no nearer to finding answers for these types of fundamental questions. What gives the mind the special capacity to create something as abstract as mathematics, and why is this seemingly human-dominated construction so powerful in describing the operations of nature?

For Plato, it was more than coincidence that our abstract mathematical concepts were able to provide powerful descriptions of nature. He constructed a philosophy in which the world of mathematics possessed a deeper reality − a world more perfect, more real than the world of the senses. For Plato, mathematics was an eternal archetype by which the universe was designed. The external world and our perceptions of it had their existence, their reason for being, in imparting to us a knowledge of mathematics.

The power of modern science comes from the ability to describe the world of nature in terms of deeper and deeper, more abstract mathematical concepts. The fundamental mysteries of mathematics, and hence the enigmas that underlie modern science, derive from the singular characteristics of the human mind, especially its ability to go beyond the world of the senses, beyond facts and observations, to form abstract concepts. The philosopher Kant, pondering this mystery in the eighteenth century, wrote that it is 'an art concealed in the depths of the human soul whose real modes of activity nature is hardly likely ever to allow us to discover'.[115]

Mathematics is a testimony to the creative character of the mind, which is not something that automatically arises from facts impinging on our senses in a mechanical fashion. No amount of sense perceptions can derive a mental class, in the same way that no number of straight lines can construct a perfect circle. They are as different from each other as infinity is from a number, as justice is from meat. They are of two entirely different categories.

8. Induction and Faith in Science

Intuitive, non-empirical leaps of the mind, creating universals from observed facts, lie at the foundation of scientific investigation. One might even say that the task of science is to find valid universals, or generalizations that make sense of our experience. Every law of physics is arrived at by a process of induction and extrapolation from a set of specific observations. Observations by themselves do not constitute science or say anything significant about the nature of the universe.

Take, for example, the different observations of water freezing: the observation that pure water freezes at zero degrees celsius during winter on a hillside; the observation of water freezing in a refrigerator on another occasion, and so on. It is not until one extrapolates to produce the general statement that pure water freezes at zero degrees celsius, that one makes a significant scientific statement. Simply listing a finite number of observations of pure water freezing does not automatically lead to something scientifically meaningful.

In fact, no amount of experiments or observations can prove that pure water freezes at zero degrees; one would need to observe water freezing under every possible circumstance, clearly an infinite number of times, before one could make the statement with absolute certainty. There will always be a point at which the scientist performs a leap of faith in devising his or her theories. Every law in physics entails such an inductive generalization, and thus involves going beyond the given facts, and no scientific theory is ever conclusively proved to be true in this sense. Every subsequent observation of pure water freezing at zero degrees celsius will no doubt strengthen the belief that water freezes at zero degrees celsius, but there will be no absolute proof of such a statement.

There are some conditions in which pure water will be observed to freeze at a different temperature, such as water freezing at the top of a mountain, which will appear to falsify the statement. This need not undermine belief in the theory, but the scientist may seek to revise an ancillary assumption and qualify the statement. As already discussed, there is no automatic way of deciding the matter – the scientist must make a decision based on his or her prior knowledge, experience and convictions. A good scientist will be led intuitively to the conclusion that another parameter is important, such as atmospheric pressure, in explaining the apparent anomaly. After perhaps performing some experiments that confirm the pressure of water to be an important parameter in determining its freezing point, the scientist will be able to make a revised statement: pure water freezes at zero degrees celsius *at standard atmospheric pressure*. Only a finite number of experiments can be performed before the scientist makes a leap of faith to produce a valid generalization about nature – a law of physics.

Every law of science must have an inherent belief content if it is to describe something meaningful about the world of nature. Newton, for example, must have postulated a link between the strength of a force applied to an object and its subsequent acceleration after making a few observations and experiments on the motion of objects. A good scientist like Newton would not have needed many of these 'facts' before arriving intuitively at his second law of motion, which states that the acceleration of an object is directly proportional to the force applied to it. A poor scientist may require many more 'facts' before the leap of faith to such a universal law can be made. A truly creative leap of faith is made by only a few gifted scientists, but a good scientist will always be characterized by a high degree of conviction in his or her theory. The success of science depends directly on the degree of faith that scientists have in their theories.

Significant theories require a greater degree of faith content in their construction than insignificant ones. A good example is Newton's first law of motion, which states that an object will remain at rest or in a state of uniform motion unless acted upon by an external force. This law embodies the concept of inertia, contradicting the former Aristotelian notion that the motion of an object was only sustained by the continued application of an external force. What observations did Newton make to derive his theory? This first law of motion is unverifiable: since there are always forces acting on the motion of objects under observation, such as wind resistance, gravitational forces and so on, it would have been an impossible feat for Newton to observe the motion of an object with no forces acting upon it. His first law of motion is a statement of faith, an abstraction of the mind. It was conceived by Newton as a thought experiment, where no direct observations could be used to derive it. A lesser scientific mind would not have had the high degree of faith required for such an imaginative construction, and yet this unverifiable, non-empirical law turns out to be one of the foundation stones of modern physics.

No theory important to the development of science can be formulated solely in terms of the facts and logical inferences that form a positivist's conception of science. Faith underlies scientific progress. To give another example, there is no guarantee that any of our present laws of physics are valid on the other side of the universe, or were the same in the past as they are now. There is no way of stating with certainty that the laws of physics do not change in time, or change according to a position in space. There are no experiments we could perform to test this, but the assumption of universality in the laws of physics is a fundamental prerequisite for the practice of any science. All important advances in modern astronomy are founded upon such a belief, and it is hardly ever questioned. Yet it is a gigantic leap of faith to believe that generalizations about the universe made by some mortal creatures on an insignificantly small planet are valid across the entire universe, both in space and time.

Science progresses through revising prior beliefs. There is no definitive way in which one theory can be proved to be better than any other; one theory may be confirmed by more observations than another, it may not clash with observations that a previous theory clashed with, yet there is no certainty that it is a better theory. Judging between rival theories involves an act of faith, and no amount of evidence can completely eliminate this belief content.

There are some beliefs, however, which are difficult to revise, since they themselves underlie scientific investigation. They may be called instinctive beliefs. One such is the belief in the law of causality: that the universe can be understood in terms of causal connections. There is no need here to stress the primary role played by the law of causality in science; without it, our different perceptions of the universe would remain disparate and unconnected, and no science could be constructed. The law of causality enables us to connect observations, such as the observation of the temperature of pure water dropping to zero degrees celsius, and of that water freezing. It is clear that if we were unable to state that the temperature of the water caused it to freeze, no science would be possible. Our belief in causal connections in the universe is not only a precondition for all scientific investigation, but is necessary for our sanity and rationality. Yet as Hume demonstrated in the eighteenth century, an empirically dominated philosophy of science leads to the nonsensical position of doubting our belief in the existence of causal connections.

Hume distinguished two different components of causality. If a cause, C, is said to have an effect, E, it is implied that whenever C occurs, E will also occur. Hume states that the two events are 'contiguous' with one another, that they are somehow related. The second aspect of causation he refers to as 'succession': events follow each other in a certain order, that is, E follows C.[116] He goes on to state, however, that it is conceivable that events can be caused without being either contiguous or successive. He concludes that there must be another factor involved in the idea of causation, and this he refers to as 'necessary causation'.[117] This aspect of causation not only means that E follows C, but that there is a 'necessary' link between the two, a definite reason why E follows C. Something causes E to follow C, without which it is possible that on some occasions C may follow E. Although it is perfectly natural to assume that there is a necessary connection forcing E to follow C, Hume becomes sceptical at this point. Can one observe such a link empirically, that is, in terms of sensory information? If the operation of cause and effect is scrutinized more and more closely, there will be some point at which the alleged link between the cause and effect becomes invisible, that is, non-sensory. The connection is only apparent.

Consider the example of two billiard balls colliding. If a moving billiard ball strikes a stationary one, at what point can one observe the first billiard ball causing the stationary ball to move? Can one obtain indisputable empirical evidence proving that the first billiard ball caused the subsequent motion of the second billiard ball? If we filmed the collision, and slowed down the replay so that we could examine it frame by frame, what kind of evidence would we have connecting the motion of one billiard ball to the other? We would have a succession of separate pictures whose order could be changed or reversed – once the collision has occurred, where is the necessary connection between each frame of film and the next? An inference, existing only in our minds, connects the contents of one frame to its successor. This type of link is non-empirical and lies at the foundation of our belief in causation.

Hume described these gaps in our thinking with remarkable clarity. He concludes that 'objects have no discoverable connexion together; nor is it from any other principle but custom operating upon the imagination, that we can draw any inference from the appearance of one to the existence of another'.[118] In other words, by a process of mere habit we impose a link between E and C where there is none. Causality, for a strict empiricist, must ultimately be a piece of metaphysics, or non-empirical nonsense. If causality is an invalid theory, however, so is science, since all science assumes the law of causality. It is clear that causality is in fact a primary belief, and that while one may attempt to doubt it theoretically, in practice it is impossible to do so and still make sense of our experience. The belief in causality is instinctive.

Another example of an instinctive belief underlying science is the belief in the existence of a world external to the mind. This belief was also doubted in Hume's philosophy. Perhaps one is dreaming. Perhaps the external world, along with all its objects and people, is a figment of one's imagination. What empirical evidence is there that can prove the existence of a world beyond one's consciousness? Is there an experiment one can perform to test such a belief? Again, as in the case of the belief in causality, there is no indisputable empirical proof that the external world is not a figment of one's imagination. Hume concludes that this belief, too, is an outcome of mere habit, and nothing more. There is no question of anything at all being meaningful without this belief.

To date, no argument in philosophical discourse has shown the sceptic's position to be invalid. It is logically tenable, yet quite unbelievable. What the sceptic has succeeded in demonstrating is that belief in the existence of a world external to our minds cannot be a proven empirical fact, and that it rests on a primary instinctive faith. Again, faith precedes reason: before any reasoning about the nature of the world can take place, one must believe it to exist. Belief in the existence in an external world is not something rational, it is pre-rational. The scepticism of a strict empiricist demonstrates very clearly that the edifice of science is grounded on primary, instinctive beliefs, and that there appears to be no way of achieving empirical certainty.

Another example of such beliefs, pre-rational and vital to the enterprise of science, is the fundamental laws of logic. The laws known as the principle of non-contradiction and the principle of excluded middle are two such laws. Aristotle was one of the first to present these laws of logic as a fundamental pre-condition to all rational discourse. The law of non-contradiction states that a proposition cannot be both true and false at the same time, and the law of excluded middle states that such a proposition must then be either true or false. All rational thought depends on the validity of these two fundamental laws of logic. It is clear that they cannot be rationally proved or disproved, since they themselves are incorporated in every rational discourse or enquiry. Every attempt at disproving them will employ them, and every form of human reasoning relies on them; to even doubt that they are true uses a notion of propositions being either true or false. They, like our belief in causality or our belief in the existence of a world external to our minds, are acts of faith – beliefs that have grown out of our experience in a pre-rational way. These primary, instinctive beliefs lie beyond the reach of reason and science. They are, rather, the very soil in which scientific knowledge grows.

Faith is an irreducible facet of human nature, and the act of believing cannot be negated. If one states that 'all beliefs are illusions', one is then forced to admit that this statement itself expresses a belief, and hence is self-defeating. Not only does every thought carry with it an inherent belief content, but it occurs against a background of prior beliefs. Human nature is not a blank tablet upon which experience or observations are written. Belief in the law of causation, in the existence of a world beyond our minds, and in the fundamental laws of logic, illustrates that faith is indispensable to science.

The pursuit of scepticism can only be taken so far. Michael Polanyi has suggested that there is a logical equivalence between the act of affirmation, and that of contradiction:

> Suppose somebody says 'I believe p' where p stands for 'planets move along elliptic orbits', or else for 'all men are mortal'. And I reply 'I doubt p'. This may be taken that I contradict p, which could be expressed by 'I believe not p' . . . It is immediately apparent that an expression of contradictory doubt 'I believe not-p' is of the same kind of character as the affirmation 'I believe p' which calls it into question. For between p and not-p there is no other difference than they refer to different matters of fact. 'I believe not-p' could stand for the allegation that planets move along orbits which are not elliptical.[119]

This suggests that the act of believing is not negated when a statement is rejected, but that faith is instead transferred. Polanyi goes on to cite examples of the logical equivalence between affirmation and contradiction in the history of science, where scientific progress was made by proving something to be impossible, that is, by contradicting it. In mathematics, the squaring of a circle or the trisection of an angle by aid of a ruler and compass were proved to be impossible, and this helped to advance progress in mathematics. In physics, the second law of thermodynamics – which states the impossibility of converting energy back into its original form once it has been dissipated – explained why the many attempts to design perpetual motion machines had failed. There are many similar examples in science of theories being formulated in negative form, proving something to be impossible, and having a positive result.

To say I disbelieve statement p is equivalent to saying I believe statement p not to be true. But there is no by-passing the act of faith by being sceptical. If one says 'I doubt p', this is equivalent to saying 'I believe p is not proven'. There is always a belief content in our thinking, and the positivist attempt to eliminate the element of faith from science arises from a misunderstanding of science and the way human minds do their thinking. Not only is every statement made against a background of convictions, but all statements that express a judgement contain an irreducible belief content.

Faith and deductive reasoning are like two sides of the coin of human thinking: without certain basic beliefs, no deductive chains of logic can be used; yet without chains of logic, no conclusions can be drawn. Michael Polanyi referred to the beliefs that underlie scientific investigation as 'tacit knowledge'.[120] The relationship between formal reasoning (deductive logic) and tacit knowledge can be likened to the relationship between an object in the foreground of a photograph and background objects. One cannot examine the foreground and background at the same time; while the foreground object is being examined, it is set into relief with respect to the background. Likewise, one can focus one's thoughts on a particular subject, but only by setting it in relief against background thoughts, which themselves must remain unexamined while one concentrates on the subject in question.

The mind engages in formal, explicit reasoning, which is apparent to us like the tip of an iceberg. Yet, the formal processes of the mind only emerge out of a vast, hidden, background way of thinking. The distinction between the tacit and the formal parts of our thinking can be understood by analogy with a telescope; our foreground thoughts may be likened to the observations we make through the telescope, while our background convictions are represented by the telescopic apparatus. Just as we cannot observe the telescope while looking through it, we cannot examine our background convictions while using them. Moreover, it is only 'through' our background convictions that new 'observations' can be made.

Scientific reasoning is a process of jumping back and forth between tacit and focal knowledge. There is always a tacit part to our thinking, an unspecified, unproven part of our knowledge. In Polanyi's words:

> We cannot ultimately specify the grounds (either metaphysical or logical or empirical) upon which we hold that our knowledge is true. Being committed to such grounds, dwelling in them, we are projecting ourselves to what we believe to be true from or through these grounds. We cannot therefore see what they are. We cannot look at them since we are looking with them. They therefore remain indeterminate. The very process of tacit integration, which we have found so ubiquitous, is, when we turn our attention directly upon it . . . also indeterminate, unspecifiable.[121]

Background convictions are inherent in foreground analysis. Scientific investigation consists of a continuous, mutually dependent process of reasoning and believing, woven together by intuitive leaps of the imagination. There are residual elements to theories, and tacit dimensions to our knowledge, that can never be fully articulated. Rules and procedures capture a part of the scientific process, but only a very small part of it. Science breathes the air of faith, without which it would decay into a jumble of meaningless procedures and observations.

9. Faith in the Unity and Rationality of Nature

A fundamental spiritual precondition for science is faith in the intelligibility of nature. The belief that there is an order or unity in nature, however imperfectly conceived by human minds, is a corner-stone of scientific knowledge, and it has been expressed in different ways throughout human history. It can be seen in the Pythagorean image of nature vibrating to musical harmonies; the Platonic idea of nature designed after archetypal forms; the Islamic conception of the universe embedded in layers of light; the Renaissance image of nature being written like a book, and many more. All these conceptions of the universe discern the pattern of an underlying order and unity. Without such a faith, scientific investigation would crumble into a meaningless set of observations and tests, which by themselves are of no significance.

The belief that science uncovers order in nature, then, imbues scientific enterprise with meaning. One can theoretically doubt nature's rationality, as Hume did when he questioned the law of causality and the existence of a world external to our minds. May not the law of gravity be an illusion? Could it not be that every time we drop an apple and observe it falling to the ground, we are observing a mere coincidence, and is there not a finite probability that next time we release an apple, it will rise upwards? There is clearly no guarantee that science uncovers genuine truths about the universe. But a faith in the rationality and order of the universe tells us that it does. Similarly, there is no guarantee that our minds are capable of deciphering the order of nature, even if it were certain that it existed. But a belief in both an order in nature and the ability of human nature to understand it are fundamental to science, even though no amount of scientific discovery can verify these beliefs beyond all doubt.

Historically, faith in the unity of nature and our ability to uncover it was linked to religion, and the interdependence between the notions of truth, meaning and unity. Truth is a primary, irreducible concept for human beings. Every attempt at defining or denying it will inevitably employ some notion of truth, as for instance in Nietzsche's attempt to dismiss it as a mistaken notion: 'Truth is the kind of error without which a certain species of life could not live.'[122] In trying to show that truth is a mistaken idea, a falsehood, even Nietzsche tacitly uses a notion of truth; if something is false, then presumably something else must be true. Without the notion of truth there can be no error, and Nietzsche's statement is therefore self-defeating. One cannot be independent of the notion of truth, or objective about it. Our ability to reason is founded on our capacity to distinguish truth from falsehood – on having the notion of truth in our minds. Truth is a spiritual instinct in human nature.

Integral to the notion of truth is the search to find it. The minds of human beings appear to be constantly moving along a series of truths, and within every truth there appears a notion of a yet higher truth, and so on, reaching out to the concept of an ultimate truth. This provides the spiritual foundation for science, and the search for ultimate truths is essential also to other human endeavours. It underlies the nature of religion.

One might attempt to be sceptical about a search for truth, particularly ultimate truths, and ask why we should search for it. But this question implies that it might be better not to search for truth – that is, an alternative exists which is in some way superior to searching for truth, in some sense more meaningful, amounting, in fact, to a deeper truth. Thus one is inevitably caught up in the search one tries to negate. The only way to reject the notion of truth and the search after truth is to be unconscious, to reach the state of mental nullity. We can flee from the notion of truth by responding only to the senses: by becoming the kind of human being modelled by empiricists. By saturating our minds with sense information, we eliminate the notion of truth from our minds. By becoming the object of the behaviourist's study (not the behaviourist himself, who has very definite notions of truth) we can escape the notion of truth. If we act mechanically and passively, responding to input sensations like a robot, the notion of truth can be eliminated from our minds. In such a state, the acquisition of all kinds of knowledge – scientific, religious, artistic, and so on – is impossible. The moment we allow ourselves to be conscious, to think, the notion of truth appears. It is non-empirical and pre-rational in character, and yet it provides the ground upon which knowledge is built.

The notion of truth is closely related to what we understand as meaning. One cannot imagine something as being true, without associating some kind of meaning with it. One cannot deny meaning in the same way that one cannot reject the notion of truth. Every attempt at defining or denying meaning will inevitably employ some prior notion of meaning. Human beings are essentially truth-seeking, meaning-seeking creatures.

Both science and religion involve searching after ultimate truths. Since faith in order and unity in the universe involves a commitment to an ultimate truth, it is essentially religious in character. The nature of ultimate truth is that it is one: there cannot be two independent ultimate truths in the universe. Because science and religion share a commitment to finding universal truths, there exists a natural unity between them. Both are committed to uncovering deeper and deeper meanings, and throughout history progress in science was greatly inspired by religious visions of the universe. Thinkers like Pythagoras, Aristotle, Kepler, Descartes and Newton were rationalists in the religious sense, with all their discoveries being naturally integrated within religious beliefs. Einstein, commenting on this religious dimension to science, wrote as follows:

> Science can only be created by those thoroughly imbued with the aspiration towards truth and understanding. This source of feeling, however, springs from the sphere of religion. To this there also belongs the faith in the possibility that the regulations valid for the world of

existence are rational, that is, comprehensible to reason. I cannot conceive of a genuine scientist without that profound faith. The situation may be expressed by an image: Science without religion is lame, religion without science is blind.[123]

This expresses what every genuine scientist experiences, that the rationality of the universe and an aspiration towards finding truth are religious feelings, and that they underlie the foundation of science. Science breathes the air of religious convictions, without which it would choke on a self-defeating form of nihilism. It is rooted in religious ground, and if uprooted from this ground, it loses vigour and ultimately decays into a jumble of meaningless facts. Michael Polanyi has referred to the contradiction arising from secular scepticism about the spiritual foundations of science as a form of 'intellectual subterfuge'.[124] He writes:

> Scientific inquiry is accordingly a dynamic exercise of the imagination and is rooted in commitments and beliefs about the nature of things. It is a fiduciary act. It is far from scepticism in itself. It depends upon firm beliefs. Nor should it ever give rise to scepticism. Its ideal is the discovery of coherence and meaning in that which we believe exists; it is not the reduction of everything to a meaningless jumble of atoms or accidentally achieved equilibrium of forces.[125]

There is another link between unity and truth that underlies the scientific enterprise, and it involves the nature of facts. What is a fact? When does a fact become a fallacy? The positivist notion is that facts are hypotheses that are proven to be true, and are independent of acts of faith. But facts, as already discussed, cannot be separated from a background world-view, because they need selection and interpretation. Indeed, facts are inseparable from social consensus, because a fact is a shorthand way of referring to something that the community has tacitly agreed to be near-certain knowledge. Facts are beliefs which most people in society hold with near-certainty; they are not objective truths independent of belief content, but they rest on beliefs that are commonly shared in society. Conversely, fallacies are related to propositions about which no social agreement can be obtained.

The validity of facts can sometimes derive from the authority of the institution or group that upholds them. In such a case, society collectively agrees to invest the statements of an individual or institution with the same near-certainty as facts of inter-subjective experience. Thus, not only is a fact related to universally shared experiences, but it can also be related to the social authority of the group or individual who states it.

These points can be illustrated by examining the belief that the planet earth is central to the universe, as it existed both before and after the Copernican revolution. Before Copernicus, the fact of the sun moving around the earth was an indisputable truth, believed universally with near-certainty. It was a fact that was amply demonstrated by observation and experience: all agreed that by simply looking up at the sky, one could see the sun moving around the earth. Not only was there this evidence, but it was a fact supported by biblical verse and ancient Greek text (from Ptolemy and Aristotle), authorities that were given the status of communicating objective truths. But after Copernicus, as the implications of his theory were absorbed, the sun's motion around the earth appeared to some to be an optical illusion. The sight of the sun moving around the earth was just as easily explainable in terms of the earth moving around the sun. Here, the new astronomy sided with a more esoteric explanation, one that was less readily confirmed by the senses. It took more than a century for the old geocentric fact to become a fallacy, and before it could do so, the authority of the Church and ancient Greek science had to be rejected. It was not until Church authorities tacitly agreed to interpret the relevant scriptural verse allegorically, and unquestioned assent to ancient Greek authority in matters of science was overturned, that the fact of the centrality of the earth became a fallacy.

A fact was thus translated into a fallacy by universal social consent. This depends on either finding a universally shared subjective experience, or reaching a collective decision to empower an individual or group to make statements about objective truth. In either case, objective truths are dependent on social consensus. It is not until a fact bears the imprint of human purposes and values, the signs of intuitive leaps of faith, that it is useful to science.

Science, therefore, entails an aspiration towards searching after truth, faith in the unity and rationality of the universe, and belief in the power of human minds to capture a description of nature's order. Moreover, good scientists feel an obligation to remain open to self-criticism; to submit their work to the scrutiny of other scientists; to report their work honestly; to take moral responsibility for their work, and conduct it in a spirit of service to humanity; and to co-operate with other scientists in a spirit of mutual trust.

Science requires respect. It is not until the scientist respects the search for truth that progress can be made. The psychologist Erich Fromm stresses this in the following way: 'Objectivity does not mean detachment, it means respect; that is, the ability not to distort and to falsify things, persons and oneself.'[126] It is clear that all these spiritual preconditions for scientific investigation are self-imposed, and that these individual moral commitments are inherent in a scientist's faith.

Science also requires reverence for the laws of nature, a feeling that is not unique to scientific investigation. Michael Polanyi has written: 'We need reverence to perceive greatness, even as we need a telescope to observe spiral nebulae.'[127] The values of a reverence for truth, faith in our reasoning faculty, faith in nature's unity, and so on, which are of crucial importance in guiding the scientist in his or her work, are not empirical or rational, but spiritual. They have more in common with religious faith than with impersonal empirical observations. In short, science is founded on human values, and on spiritual ideals.

The great breakthroughs in the history of science united different parts of the universe previously thought to be separate, and as a result provided a more coherent and unified picture of the universe. This is true for Pythagoras uniting music with mathematics; or Newton proposing an equivalence between planetary orbits and terrestrial mechanics; or Maxwell uniting the electric and magnetic forces; or Einstein bringing inertial and gravitational forces together as one force. All these breakthroughs in science are acts of finding hidden links, and it is a fundamental characteristic of all genuine scientific truth that it is unifying. As Aristotle noted 2,500 years ago, the power and character of science lies in its unity and universality. Every hidden link discovered by science must be preceded by an unwavering faith in the unity and universality of the laws of nature.

In its most basic form, science involves us in making sense of our experience. This definition of science captures its essential spirit, much more so than the positivist's reduction of science into a series of formal logical procedures and impersonal observations. One cannot censor out the meaning component in our observation of facts, and the experience of meaning is fundamental to science. When a scientific breakthrough unites two seemingly disparate phenomena, such as making electric and magnetic forces one, it moves from one set of meanings to a deeper set of meanings – from one set of truths to a deeper set of truths.

10. The Search for Universal Meaning

The analogy used by the seventeenth-century pioneers of science, that it is a method of deciphering the Book of Nature, helps to illustrate the fundamental role played by meaning in science. Comparing scientific discovery with the process of finding meaning in a written text shows that the nature of science is grounded in the meaning it conveys.

No individual word can by itself supply the meaning of a sentence. The reduction of a book into a collection of unrelated words would destroy its whole character and filter out its meaning content. The meaning of a sentence is somehow intuitively extracted from a collection of individual words – the human mind performs the holistic, creative act that combines all the words together, and yet somehow goes beyond them to form an entirely different category, a sentence. No collection of separate words can capture the character of a sentence. It is futile to state that a sentence is no more than a grouping of words, or words no more than a collection of letters. Likewise, it is futile to describe science as a collection of facts, or our understanding of nature as no more than a bundle of sense-perceptions. Meaning is extracted from the facts of nature, just as the meaning of sentences is imaginatively constructed from the words that compose them. A fact on its own is about as useful as a word on its own.

The popular image that science only deals with 'brute facts' is comparable to the idea that there is no connection between individual 'letters' and 'words' in the Book of Nature, and amounts to more than a simple misreading. Strict empiricism would only read the Book of Nature letter by letter – in effect, discouraging one from reading the book as a whole. There can be no definitive proof for the belief that nature carries wider meanings and purposes of which the individual facts form a natural part. There is no proof at any stage where science relates facts together to form the laws of nature that these laws themselves are not purely illusory. The universal character of scientific laws reinforces the notion that nature is like a book, carrying overall meanings and purposes – it does not prove this with absolute certainty.

A book is approached with the expectation that it will convey something useful and meaningful. No one picks up a book assuming that it contains meaningless dabs of ink on its pages – least of all a scientist. Moreover, a good book demands the full attention of its reader, and involves him or her in a riveting search from page to page, piecing together an ever-unfolding mystery. There is no attempt to dispassionately observe the ink on the page, censoring out any meanings that may occur to the reader. Moreover, it is quite natural to enquire after the character of the author – to seek to understand the mind of the author.

The greatest scientists of the past have conducted their science with a profound conviction that there is a Book of Nature, and that there are universal meanings behind our experience of the world. They expected to find meanings, and only by working in this frame of mind were they able to make important advances. Conversely, the work of mediocre scientists may be likened to those who attempt to read the Book of Nature letter by letter, forever pausing to look up word-definitions in a dictionary.

Since it is in the nature of science to progress along a path of deeper and deeper meanings, it follows that the whole enterprise is anchored in faith in ultimate meanings, which are essentially religious in character. It was no accident that the seventeenth-century pioneers of modern science modelled their ideas about the Book of Nature on the Book of Revelation. If scientific truth is genuinely universal, it will necessarily assume a religious dimension. There can be no pretence of being able to filter out religious meaning from science – an impossibility. To quote Michael Polanyi once more:

Modern science cannot properly be understood to tell us

that the world is meaningless and pointless, that it is absurd. The supposition that it is absurd is a modern myth, created imaginatively from the clues produced by a profound misunderstanding of what science and knowledge are and what they require, a misunderstanding spawned by positivistic leftovers in our thinking and by allegiance to the false ideal of objectivity from which we have been unable to shake ourselves quite free. These are the stoppages in our ears that we must pull out if we are ever once more to experience the full range of meanings possible to man.[128]

The act of faith within science plays a similar role to that which it plays in religion: 'As ye have faith, so shall your powers and blessings be';[129] and 'if thou canst believe, all things are possible to him that believeth' (Mark 9:23). Faith is not only the spiritual prerequisite for moving mountains in religion, but it is also a spiritual precondition for solving great problems in science.

William James, the philosopher and psychologist writing around the turn of the century, noted that faith is an irreducible facet of human nature:

It is almost incredible that men who are themselves working philosophers should pretend that any philosophy can be, or ever has been, constructed without the help of personal preference, belief, or divination. How have they succeeded in so stultifying their sense for the living facts of human nature as not to perceive that every philosopher, or man of science either, whose initiative counts for anything in the evolution of thought, has taken his stand on a sort of dumb conviction that the truth must lie in one direction rather than another, and a sort of preliminary assurance that his notion can be made to work; and has borne his best fruit in trying to make it work? These mental instincts in different men are the spontaneous variations upon which the intellectual struggle for existence is based. The fittest conceptions survive, and with them the names of their champions shining to all futurity. The coil is all about us, struggle as we may. The only escape from faith is mental nullity.[130]

Not only is faith inescapable, but James describes a certain type of faith as its 'own verification', by which he means that the act of commitment is the only route. He draws the analogy of someone stranded on a mountainside, whose only route to survival lies in making a leap to a nearby ledge. If no leap is made, the person will die of cold. James emphasizes that this individual may never have made such a leap before, and the only way of discovering whether he can make the leap is to try it. With this kind of leap of faith no amount of prior experience can determine its outcome; in fact, prior experience is only likely to inhibit one from making the leap. There is all to gain, and nothing to lose. The parallel with traditional religious faith is obvious, but this example also captures the character of courageous leaps of faith in science. One can always find a way of doubting the foundations of science; at every stage there is the opportunity to doubt the spiritual ground upon which science is founded, and this scepticism will produce hesitancy. Yet it is only when courageous leaps of faith are made that extraordinary scientific advances result. The larger the leaps of faith, the greater the advances are likely to be. There is always a risk element in science.

The greatest scientists were people of extraordinary faith. They possessed devout confidence in nature's unity and rationality, and this inner conviction is inseparable from their genius. Newton wrote:

> I do not know what I may appear to the world; but to myself I seem to have been only a boy, playing on a seashore, and diverting myself, in now and then finding a smoother pebble or a prettier shell than ordinary, whilst the great ocean of truth lay all undiscovered before me.[131]

The act of discovering prettier and smoother pebbles, that is, of discovering more and more unified laws of nature, relied upon a conviction of truth and unity without which each pebble on the beach, each theory in science, would have been indistinguishable.

Newton's conviction that an ocean of truth underlay scientific investigation gave his work a depth that makes that of lesser scientists appear superficial. Two fields of knowledge, which to others had appeared unrelated – terrestrial mechanics and planetary motion, the fall of an apple and the motion of the moon – were united in a creative flash of Newton's genius.

The awe and humility with which a scientist of the stature of Newton looked upon the world can be thought of as a child-like fascination with the wonder of nature. Newton considered science to be an infinitely small part of a wider truth. The great scientist's humble and child-like faith in nature's order and unity recalls the humility enjoined on followers of religion: 'No one can see the Kingdom of God unless he is born again' (John 3:3).

Of course Newton had his conflicts. His disputes with other scientists such as Robert Hook and Gottfried Leibniz have been well documented.[132] But it is his humility before the great mysteries of nature that is particularly striking. It is entirely at odds with the positivist claim that 'everything is in principle known'. For the great scientist, everything is genuinely mysterious. These characteristics were also unmistakable in Einstein, who regarded the fact that nature was comprehensible to human reasoning as nothing short of a miracle:

> The very fact that the totality of our sense experiences is such that by means of thinking (operations with concepts, and the creation and use of definite functional relations between them, and the coordination of sense experiences to these concepts) it can be put in order, this fact is one which leaves us in awe, but which we shall never understand. One might say 'the eternal mystery of the world is its comprehensibility'.[133]

Elsewhere Einstein stated that the 'most incomprehensible thing about the universe is that it is comprehensible'.[134] No amount of empirical evidence can produce this feeling, a feeling that underlies the whole scientific enterprise.

The search to capture what can only be regarded as glimpses of nature's order and unity entailed for Einstein a mystical faith.

Science was looked upon as a religious experience:

> Whoever has undergone the intense experience of successful advances made in this domain, is moved by profound reverence for the rationality made manifest in existence. By way of the understanding he achieves a far-reaching emancipation from the shackles of personal hopes and desires, and thereby attains that humble attitude of mind towards the grandeur of reason incarnate in existence, and which in its profoundest depths, is inaccessible to man. This attitude, however, appears to me to be religious in the highest sense of the word.[135]

Here, Einstein describes an experience perfectly recognizable to religious people. The liberation from egocentric cravings; the reaching out for higher universal truths that one can only glimpse and struggle to rationalize; the 'humble attitude of mind' which characterizes such reflections and meditations – all this is shared between the genuinely scientific and the genuinely religious.

Modern positivist conceptions of science most often present it as eliminating mystery, as an enemy of faith. In a technique-dominated conception of science, little or no faith is demanded from a scientist. Tautological propositions do not require much faith; to state that all circles are round requires little faith or feeling for mystery. But it is precisely for this reason that they convey nothing of scientific significance. Their certainty inhibits their usefulness. The uncertainty, sense of mystery, and vision of unity that characterize a genuine scientist give rise to bold speculations, which are much more conducive to scientific advances than hypotheses of a tautological nature.

The prediction that light would 'bend' as it travelled in space, made long before experiment confirmed it, was a daring proposition made by Einstein, and required a high degree of faith. Not only did this proposition go against prevailing knowledge about the characteristics of light at the time it was formulated, but it arose out of a series of thought experiments – very few empirical observations were involved in its formulation. In fact, a single thought experiment lay at the foundation of Einstein's theory of general relativity.

General relativity is founded on the principle that inertial and gravitational forces are one. Einstein realized this by a simple thought experiment in which he imagined a man falling from a roof, and saw that the falling man would not himself be aware of possessing weight. He observed that if, for instance, the falling man also dropped some tools while falling, they would appear to him to be 'weightless', and thus the experience of gravity was equivalent to one's acceleration relative to other objects. Einstein later described this thought as the 'happiest thought of my life', and recalled it in the following way:

> I was sitting in a chair in the patent office at Bern when all of a sudden a thought occurred to me: 'If a person falls freely he will not feel his own weight.' I was startled. This simple thought made a deep impression on me. It impelled me toward a theory of gravitation.[136]

Einstein realized that 'therefore the observer has the right to interpret his state as at rest'.[137] Later he refined his thought experiment to involve an observer being placed in a box, and the box being pulled up by an external force – similar to the situation in an ordinary lift. As the external force is applied to the box, the observer inside it will feel a force pulling him down to the bottom of the box. There will be no way by which the observer can distinguish this pull, being caused by an external force accelerating the box upwards, from the force of gravity acting down upon him – the effect of these seemingly separate forces appears identical. This thought experiment, like the original one of the man falling from a roof, illustrated to Einstein that he could envisage a situation where the effect of gravity and an inertial force appeared to be identical, and thus led him to formulate a universal principle of equivalence.

Einstein was so confident about his thought analogy that he imagined a further embellishment. A ray of light is emitted from one side of the box to the other side while the box is being accelerated upwards. Would an observer positioned outside the box not see the ray of light bend, as it arrived on the opposite wall at a point slightly lower than the one it started with? Since there was no way of distinguishing between an inertial force and a gravitational one, would the light not also appear to bend under the presence of a gravitational field? Einstein had sufficient confidence in his simple thought experiment to predict subsequently that the path of a ray of light would appear to bend as it travelled through the gravitational fields of stars and planets. This was a courageous proposition. For centuries before, light was only believed to travel in straight lines. Einstein did not construct his theory of general relativity on any direct empirical observation of light bending; it arose from a thought experiment – using a minimum number of observations with which others were also familiar. Other people could easily have constructed similar thought experiments. In 1919, Einstein's theory was confirmed by the observation of light bending around the sun's gravitational field during a solar eclipse.

We should note here the complementary role that observations and theory play in science. Einstein's faith in his gravitational theory was proved successful only by experimental tests. Performing experiments is crucial to scientific investigation, but the creative role of the mind in all this is primary, not secondary. Scientific investigation involves us putting something to the test, but unlike the positivist, the scientist's experience tells him or her that this 'test' cannot be defined with great precision, and does not rely on methodology. Putting something to the test in science requires the personal skill and judgement of scientists, and is extremely difficult to define. The well-known test 'by their fruits ye shall know them' plays a similar role in identifying genuine religious believers, as observations and experiments do in helping the scientist find objective truths. None of this can be defined with great precision, or be independent of personal commitments and judgements. By emphasizing the role of observations and experiments in an impersonal sense, the positivist obscures the creative role of the human mind in science.

For Einstein the type of unity discovered in his thought experiment was a sign of a deeper, hidden equivalence. His intuition that this equivalence between the effect of gravity and an accelerating force hid a deeper law of physics drew heavily upon his faith that the whole universe was a unity. The power of the general theory of relativity, as with many other great theories of science, is that it is based on understanding the universe to possess a greater underlying unity. The daring prediction that light would bend in a gravitational field came from Einstein's deep confidence that nature organized itself in a way that was intelligible to the mind – so much so, that an abstract thought experiment could lead to such decisive and significant conclusions.

Confirmation that this kind of faith was an important factor in Einstein's science can be found in his comment about uniting gravitational forces with electromagnetic forces, a goal that later dominated his scientific work: 'For years it has been my greatest ambition to resolve the duality of natural laws into unity.'[138] It is a search that is still continuing, indeed a major goal of modern physics. On another occasion, referring to his belief that the constants of nature associated with the laws of physics were not accidental but reflected some deeper underlying order of the universe, Einstein wrote:

> I would like to state a theorem which at present cannot be based upon anything more than upon a faith in the simplicity, i.e. intelligibility of nature: there are no arbitrary constants of this kind.'[139]

Einstein's thought experiments show that the mind is constantly going beyond sense-perceptions, and it is precisely this ability that makes dramatic advances in science. Einstein's work was very different from mere tautologies, such as 'all circles are round'. It required faith in non-empirical, pre-rational intuitions, and faith in the unity of nature; it highlights the spiritual character of science.

Many breakthroughs in physics have come through thought experiments. Their lasting impact on scientific knowledge shows that the foundation of science is not so much facts, but the creative ability of the mind to go beyond them. Einstein's theory of special relativity, which has advanced the progress of science so much this century, was also based on a thought experiment. Einstein recalls how, when he was sixteen, he imagined travelling at the speed of light along with a light beam, and the resulting paradox was that he would expect to see an electromagnetic wave at rest, that is, not oscillating – but it would cease to be a wave if it did not oscillate. This led him to feel something was lacking in the interpretation of Maxwell's theory, and ultimately spurred him on to develop his theory of special relativity:

> After ten years' reflection . . . from a paradox upon which I had already hit at the age of sixteen: If I pursue a beam of light with the velocity *c* (velocity of light in a vacuum), I should observe such a beam of light as a spatially oscillatory electromagnetic field at rest. However, there seems to be no such thing, whether on the basis of experience or according to Maxwell's equations. From the very beginning it seemed to me intuitively clear that, judged from the standpoint of such an observer, everything would have to happen according to the same laws as for an observer who, relative to the earth, was at rest.[140]

Einstein had intuitively recognized the founding principle of special relativity: that the laws of physics describing an electromagnetic wave such as light would have to be independent of an observer's speed relative to it. This led to the conclusion that the speed of light must be constant with respect to all frames of reference. This founding principle of special relativity was not derived from the results of the Michelson–Morely experiment, first performed in 1887, which tried to measure a difference in the speed of light along two directions moving with respect to one another. This is the mistaken assumption made in many physics text books.[141] The results of the Michelson–Morely experiment were for a long time far from conclusive. The basis upon which Einstein constructed his theory was the demand that the laws of physics be consistent and rational.

Newton's work was also characterized by thought experiments. His first law involved imagining an object travelling along a frictionless plane, continuing in a straight line unless acted upon by an external force. No frictionless plane exists; it is an imaginative construct of the mind, and yet its power in advancing scientific understanding has been considerable.

Perhaps Newton's most dramatic thought experiment was his vision of a stone thrown from the surface of the earth; he predicted that if the stone were thrown with sufficient force, it would 'orbit' around the earth. Nowhere else in science is the creative power of the mind more clearly illustrated than in this example. It took 200 years before satellites were launched to follow the trajectory that Newton had already sketched out in his mind! The power of the mind to go beyond empirical observations and postulate hidden connections, spurred on by a courageous commitment to nature's underlying rationality and unity, is clearly demonstrated by the lasting impact of such a thought experiment.

Today's general picture of modern science is a vague form of positivism, with an insistence that facts play a primary role. The scientific method is regarded as consisting largely of strict logical procedures and objective observations, which is not the picture of science shared by outstanding scientists of the past, such as Newton and Einstein. One might even venture to suggest that had Newton or Einstein attempted to restrict themselves to the kind of methodology prescribed by positivism, their scientific work would not have been possible.

Confirmation of this point is found in Einstein's remarks concerning Bertrand Russell's theory of knowledge. Einstein notes that a 'fear of metaphysics' had come to be the 'malady of contemporary empiricistic philosophizing', and says of Russell's philosophy: 'No matter how much one may admire the acute analysis which Russell has given us in his latest book on *Meaning and Truth*, it still seems to me that even there the specter of the metaphysical fear has caused some damage.'[142] Einstein notes the dangers of carrying 'Hume's critique' too far, to the point of rejecting those elements within our thinking that cannot be reduced to 'sensory raw material'.[143] He points out that important concepts in our thinking cannot be reduced to 'sense experiences', writing: 'The concepts which arise in our thought and in our linguistic expressions are all – when viewed logically – the free creations of thought which cannot inductively be gained from sense experiences.'[144] In Einstein's experience as a scientist, the kind of empiricism that lay behind much of Russell's philosophy of science was not a fair representation of how science worked.

Similar conclusions about positivism were reached by some other outstanding physicists of this century, such as Max Planck, Niels Bohr, Wolfgang Pauli and Werner Heisenberg, whose work contributed much to the development of quantum physics, which describes phenomena on the microscopic scale.

In his recollections, Werner Heisenberg records conversations that took place largely between himself, Pauli and Bohr touching on the validity of positivism as a philosophy of science.[145] Quantum physics was being formulated at precisely the same time as positivism was being presented as a formal philosophy of science, in the 1920s. It is interesting to note how Heisenberg, Bohr and Pauli distanced themselves from positivism. These physicists agreed that if their own work had been restricted to the methods of positivism, this would have prevented them from developing quantum theory.

Quantum physics incorporates many seemingly contradictory observations: when viewed by one technique, observation reveals the existence of a particle, yet in precisely the same experiment, when only the apparatus of measurement is changed, a wave is detected. The notion of objectivity, the assumption that the characteristics of an object are independent of the way we perceive them, is seriously called into question by the paradoxes of quantum physics. The idea that one can define a conceptually clear-cut method by which scientific investigation proceeds is also rejected by quantum theory. Niels Bohr said:

Positivist insistence on conceptual clarity is, of course, something I fully endorse, but their prohibition of any discussion of the wider issues, simply because we lack clear-cut enough concepts in this realm, does not seem very useful to me – this same ban would prevent our understanding quantum theory. . . . Quantum theory thus provides us with a striking illustration of the fact that we can fully understand a connection though we can only speak of it in images and parables. In this case, the images and parables are by and large the classical concepts, i.e. 'wave' and 'corpuscle'. They do not fully describe the real world and are, moreover, complementary in part, and hence contradictory. For all that, since we can only describe natural phenomena with our everyday language, we can hope to grasp the real facts by means of these images. This is probably true of all general philosophical problems and particularly of metaphysics. We are forced to speak in images and parables which do not express precisely what we mean. Nor can we avoid occasional contradictions; nevertheless, the images help us to draw nearer to the real facts. Their existence no one should deny.[146]

These comments by Bohr are instructive about the nature of science. One cannot always use clear-cut concepts in scientific investigation. In fact, when it comes to the more interesting problems in science, a scientist often grapples with the problem by using 'images and parables'. This process is not unscientific. It is only by using such means that scientists gain an understanding of problems. The more fundamental the problems are, the less precise one can be about them. It is easy to be precise about '0=0', but much more difficult to know what we mean by causality, or truth, or faith, or any other fundamental notion crucial to the advance of science. Quantum theory produces conceptual ambiguities and contradictions, since it cannot be objective: one affects the measurement while one is in the act of measuring, just as one uses a notion of truth while trying to define truth. Max Planck, whose work laid the foundation for all subsequent work in quantum physics, appreciated the limitations involved in being objective about fundamental questions. 'Science cannot solve the ultimate mystery of nature,' he wrote. 'And that is because, in the last analysis, we ourselves are a part of nature, and therefore, part of the mystery we are trying to solve.'[147]

Fundamental propositions of science thus have much in common with truths in religion – they can only be conveyed in the form of 'images and parables'. There are limits to how much of our experience can be conveyed in terms of logically precise methods – even our scientific experience.

In the Pythagorean analogy, science is like music. As with a symphony, it contains underlying themes, which are religious or spiritual, melodies of human commitments and values, crescendos of personal involvement, and counterpoints of meaning. The nature of science is not described by its 'brute facts', any more than the character of a symphony is captured by identifying its individual musical notes. The symphony evokes a response from the listener. Likewise, science draws in the enquirer, moving through layers upon layers of meaning, and involves us in a discovery of universal harmonies. At the most profound level, it is a religious experience – a mysterious connection between humanity and the cosmos.

Part Three

....

THE INNER VISION

11. The Paradoxes of Modernity

Much of the drive behind the creation of the modern impersonal world-view came from the search for a secular response to traditional religion. An impersonal view, one that denies humanity a place in the cosmos and takes away human freedom, has attempted to found science on secular mythology. It is interesting to note that empiricism has largely been advocated by philosophers such as Hume and Russell, while the leaders of scientific thought (those who most contributed to its development, such as Kepler, Newton and Einstein) were rationalists who emphasized the creative role of the mind in scientific investigation.

The advocates of positivism and empiricism over the past century were also those who supported the thesis of a state of warfare between science and religion. Bertrand Russell, for example, drew a clear distinction between the modern and the traditional world-view. The former, he stated, is largely founded on science: 'Almost everything that distinguishes the modern world from earlier centuries is attributable to science.'[148]

But the dividing line between a modern scientific world-view and a pre-modern religious one is not so clear-cut as is suggested by supporters of the warfare thesis. There are many religious elements to modern thought, and the religious world-view still permeates secular societies. According to opinion polls carried out in 1980, over ninety per cent of the British, American and German populations declared themselves to be religious.[149] The statistics also indicate that over eighty per cent of people in these countries identify themselves as Christians, but rarely go to church. What this shows is that although religion has ceased to be a visible force in modern secular societies, it strongly persists. Religion involves, for the most part, a private faith, and has long since been separated from the state. It is not capable of creating social consensus as it formerly did, but it still has strong influence. Speaking on 'The Persistence of Faith' as part of the 1990 Reith Lectures, Jonathan Sacks said: 'The Sea of Faith has neither retreated nor has there been a turn of the tide. Rather, there have been turbulences: unsettling shifts in all directions.'[150]

The most notable signs of religion in a secular society appear in times of crisis, like war. There is still a prevailing belief in our societies that 'the good must triumph in the end'; that an evil dictator must eventually fall. Likewise, there is still a belief that all forms of stealing are wrong, or that life is sacred – and this suggests that there is still a strong religious undercurrent to modern culture, and that scepticism is a theoretical disturbance on the surface of modern thought.

Modern humanity, it seems, has divided loyalties. There is a conflict between theory and practice. The vast majority of people still live according to religious ethics, but the modern mind is plagued with a scepticism that unsettles deeper religious convictions. One writer has said the predicament of modern man is that 'he can neither believe, nor be comfortable in his unbelief', and goes on to state:

> We experience tension and strain as we try desperately to hold wildly contradictory beliefs about (for instance) the nature of decision and about the status of values in a world of facts. This conflict . . . has made modern life profoundly anxious, because, in addition to the personal dilemmas that have always plagued men, we now confront a metaphysical dilemma: we cannot form a comprehensive and consistent conception of human nature, or of our place in the cosmos.[151]

Our human self-image has been caught up in the ideological struggle between a secular world-view and a traditional religious one. We are only just beginning to gain a wider perspective on some of the ideological conflicts that characterize modernity. The efforts to substitute science for religion, made from late in the last century to the middle of this one, are now beginning to seem naive. Science has limits: no amount of information can create knowledge, and no amount of knowledge can be a substitute for wisdom. Religion, on the other hand, has the acquisition of wisdom as its central concern.

We live in a society dominated by information. Everywhere we turn, we are bombarded by it; we can hope to 'digest' only a fraction of this information, and with the creative participation of our minds, to turn it into knowledge. But the task of transforming our knowledge into wisdom is much more difficult, since like our broken self-image our concept of wisdom has also undergone fragmentation. As with information, there is much 'knowledge' to acquire in the modern world. But what is it all for?

Wisdom used to be defined, in a religious sense, as the making of an inner journey, and the acquisition of God-like attributes on the way. Wisdom was previously inextricably linked to goals and purposes, to what we ultimately value. From a religious perspective, there is nothing more important than discovering our true selves, making the search to understand why we exist, and fulfilling our life-purpose – this is true wisdom. 'Modern' wisdom is still primarily related to all these values, and most of us would agree that if there is a life-purpose, it would be 'unwise' to ignore it. But there is a tendency to do precisely this in the modern world.

This century has witnessed attempts at founding societies based on the techniques and developments of science, and efforts towards finding a comprehensive scientific description of human nature. From the Marxist notion that society is regulated by the science of evolution, a competition between classes, to the world of behaviourism, science has in one form or another been conceived of as a surrogate religion. Its failures have much to teach us.

One lesson that can perhaps be learned is that pseudo-science cannot be used as a secular ideological response to traditional religious beliefs. Another lesson might be that the kind of human nature presented to us in the modern impersonal world-view does not accord with our experience of being human. Up to now, such theories have not been able to describe the distinctive qualities of mind that were needed to create these very theories in the first place, such as our capacity to reason, our creative power of abstraction, our search for truth and so on.

Another lesson to be learned from the efforts to replace religion with science is that an impersonal form of science does not naturally provide a place for human values. If the methods of such a science were wantonly applied to problems outside scientific research, then we would need to adopt a value-neutral moral position, now something of a period piece.

Value-neutralism was fashionable in the middle part of this century, particularly in the social sciences. Robert Beirstedt, a social scientist, said that 'a scientist . . . is interested not in what is right or wrong or good or evil, but only what is true or false'.[152] Value-neutralism was a philosophy that had wider implications for people outside science, since one cannot in practice draw a sharp distinction between science and non-science. Value-neutralism was associated with a 'scientific' way of behaving. Of course, this link between value-neutralism in society at large and an impersonal conception of science exists mainly on the psychological level.

The aims of value-neutralism are, of course, good ones. The concern is to preserve intellectual honesty and integrity – a condition of open-mindedness. When stated positively, it is a form of commitment. Successful science depends on scientists accepting self-imposed obligations such as respecting truth, being open to the revision of prior beliefs and theories in the light of new evidence, working in co-operation with other scientists, and so on. Such a picture of science, one that includes commitments and self-imposed obligations, is also more in harmony with our moral experience outside science. But the danger of value-neutralism is that the scientist starts to think of himself or herself *only* as a science worker who is not interested in what is right or wrong, or that non-scientists will tend to think they are being scientific when they do not concern themselves with moral questions.

Value-neutralism is a curious principle to follow. It is clearly a self-defeating one, because if one is to reject the holding of values, one is also led to reject value-neutralism, which is clearly presented as a guiding principle or value for scientific investigation. Scepticism about values can only go so far. Like many of the other inconsistencies in the modern world-view, this is a suspended form of logic where scepticism is taken as far as required to negate a traditional religious world-view, without taking it to the point of explicit self-defeat.

Most people recognize that science cannot create moral values, and most understand that science is ethically neutral. Although this is an obvious point, it has to be continually reiterated, since the abuses of science are many. From a moral perspective, science has clear limits. This limitation has sometimes been expressed by describing science as concerned with 'what is', rather than 'what should be'. Einstein expressed it in the following way:

> Knowledge of what is does not open the door directly to what should be. One can have the clearest and most complete knowledge of what is, and yet not be able to deduct from that what should be the goal of our human aspirations.[153]

Although most people would agree with this statement of Einstein, they would not necessarily share his views about what were matters of fact, and what were matters of value. In other words, there is confusion over distinguishing facts from values and a tendency to emphasize the former and minimize the latter. This tendency is very much related to a positivist world-view, in which facts, procedures and methods are emphasized at the expense of commitment, human imagination and creativity.

There are many examples of this in the modern world. The experience of Einstein can once again serve to illustrate the point. Einstein was a great peace campaigner, and he wrote hundreds of letters and articles, participated in many conferences, and gave numerous radio interviews, all promoting the idea of creating a supranational organization as the way to obtain world peace. Einstein was convinced that a form of world federal government was the only way to put an end to warfare between nation states. He was so sure of this that he wrote: 'World government is inevitable, the question that remains is: at what price?'[154] In 1947, he wrote an open letter to the United Nations, proposing a series of changes that would enable it to become the kind of supranational organization he envisaged.[155]

Underlying his peace work was a deeply held conviction in the unity of humanity. Commenting on this underlying value, Otto Nathan and Heinz Norden, who have collected and edited Einstein's papers on peace, wrote: 'Einstein was a man with an almost obsessive drive to help in what he himself once called "the greatest of all causes – good will among men and peace on earth".'[156] In the creation of a supranational organization, Einstein thought, the interests of humanity would be protected from the interests of nation states. The challenge of achieving world security was, according to Einstein, above all a question of the reorientation of human values. It was about the acquisition of a wider allegiance, one that transcended national sovereignty in favour of interests serving the world as a whole.

Apart from the political opposition Einstein encountered over his ideas (proposed at the height of the cold war period), he frequently felt the need to reiterate the role that science could play in bringing about world peace. He wrote: 'Science has brought forth this danger, but the real problem is in the minds and hearts of men.'[157] On many occasions, Einstein was misunderstood and considered to be too pessimistic. In reply, he wrote:

> I have never concluded that there is no salvation for mankind. Betterment of conditions the world over is not essentially dependent on scientific knowledge but on the fulfilment of human ideals, I believe therefore, that men like Confucius, Buddha, Jesus, and Gandhi have done more for humanity with respect to the development of ethical behaviour than science could ever accomplish.[158]

Einstein on several occasions felt the need to clarify his view that the issue of world peace was primarily a question of human values, and not a technical question. On different occasions he spoke of an imbalance in the modern world between moral concerns and intellectual or technical ones. He wrote: 'Man does not lack the intelligence to overcome the evils in society. What is lacking is his selfless, responsible dedication to the service of mankind.'[159]

Moreover, Einstein understood this over-emphasis on techniques and knowledge to be a particularly modern fault. Speaking about the world's economic and political dangers, he said:

> A realization of how great is the danger is spreading, however, among thinking people, and there is much search for means with which to meet the danger – means in the field of national and international politics, of legislation, or organisation in general. Such efforts are, no doubt, greatly needed. Yet the ancients knew something which we seem to have forgotten. All means prove but a blunt instrument, if they have not behind them a living spirit. But if the longing for the achievement of the goal is powerfully alive within us, then shall we not lack the strength to find the means for reaching the goal and for translating it into deeds.[160]

Ervin Laszlo, scientist and philosopher, participated in an international research project on human goals for the Club of Rome,[161] an organization that initiated and directed many studies on global problems. He too noted the modern tendency of replacing questions of human values with collections of facts, techniques and knowledge. After participating in various studies on global problems, Laszlo wrote a book entitled *The Inner Limits of Mankind*, whose basic theme highlighted the widespread disposition to give too much emphasis to 'outer limits', such as limited energy resources, food supplies, and so on, to the detriment of 'inner limits', that is, problems to do with outmoded human ethics and values. Laszlo states that there is a tendency to 'blame the finitude of the environment', diverting attention away from the real causes of global problems, which are our own ways of thinking:

> The blame is tacitly shifted to the nature and finitude of the environment, and engineers are scurrying to their drawing boards to redesign it here and there so that we can remain as and what we are. It is forgotten that not our world, but we human beings are the cause of our problems,

and that only by redesigning our thinking and acting, not the world around us, can we solve them.

The critical but as yet generally unrecognized issue confronting mankind is that its truly decisive limits are inner, not outer.[162]

Among the ethics that Laszlo recommends changing is the belief that 'science can solve all problems and reveal all that can be known about the human race and the world – that science discovers "facts" and they alone are what counts; values, preferences and aspirations are merely subjective and inconsequential'.[163] Moreover, Laszlo identifies these kinds of beliefs as singularly modern, and states that a person who holds them is 'a truly modern person, the ideal and perhaps the envy of most of the world's peoples. *And he has become a serious threat to the future of mankind.*'[164] Like Einstein, Laszlo points to the wisdom contained in the world's spiritual traditions as an antidote to an overdose of modernity.

There is of course a technical side to global problems, and it should not be ignored. The important point here is that the truly decisive limits are inner ones. Just as it is easy to fall into the trap of regarding science as primarily dominated by logical procedures and empirical methods, there is a danger of thinking of global problems mainly in technical terms. One might, for instance, easily be misled into taking the view that global problems are largely characterized by complexity: that our difficulty in solving them is rooted in our ignorance of all the causes involved, in not having all the facts or information before us. Solving world problems therefore seems to be a largely technical task involving writing ever more complicated and sophisticated computer programs. The limitation of this approach, however, is that it misses the human element. However powerful the computer simulations may be, they cannot be used to understand the moral dimension of global problems. They cannot 'simulate' the ethic of selflessness in the service of humanity, or quantify the human aspirations and fears that lead to nationalism or terrorism.

There is another aspect to the divorce between facts and values today, and it is the problem of controlling the inventions of science. Bertrand Russell recognized the danger of losing sight of human goals and purposes while emphasizing 'scientific skill' alone. He said that the consequence of such thinking would be that the applications of science would be dependent on chance:

> Unlike religion, [science] is ethically neutral: it assures men that they can perform wonders, but does not tell them what wonders to perform. In this way it is incomplete. In practice, the purposes to which scientific skill will be devoted depend largely on chance. The men at the head of the vast organizations which it necessitates can, within limits, turn it this way or that as they please.[165]

The application of science is not something that science itself can be faulted for. But our approach is considerably weakened by the kind of moral scepticism implicit in the impersonal view of science. We cannot and must not be value-neutral about the applications of science. The loss of control over scientific inventions might easily result from concentrating on methods and techniques at the expense of values. Of course, many other factors come into play here. Scientific research and technology are closely tied to economic considerations, which in our liberal democratic societies often seem to lie beyond the control of individuals or governments. Many unacceptable applications of scientific research also originate with governments, who make science the servant of warfare. But whatever or whoever determines the applications of science, the problem is compounded by a philosophy that regards science as impersonal, and a society that admires the skill involved in producing bigger and more powerful machines, without addressing questions of moral responsibility. It is all too easy for scientists to separate themselves from the applications of their work. These dangers are made more menacing by an impersonal conception of science, where facts are clearly separated from values, and there are two different groups of people in society, one dealing with facts, the other restricting themselves to values.

The uses and applications of science in society might be beneficial or destructive, and value-neutralism tends to encourage an atmosphere where the outcome is ruled by chance. In practice, the application of science will depend on the whims of powerful people, as science becomes a tool by which individuals or organizations maintain or expand their domination. If one takes seriously the common view that a human being is an inherently selfish and aggressive animal, then there is every reason to expect the powerful 'animals' on whom the applications of science depend to direct it to their own selfish ends, impervious to its effect on others. With every scientific advance, there is the accompanying fear that it could be used for socially destructive purposes. The dangers of a nuclear holocaust, of genetic manipulation, and of environmental catastrophes are all accentuated by value-neutralism, because it appears to provide a pseudo-scientific platform for an ethic of selfishness. This accounts for much of the helplessness and despair of the modern world, and is the cause of much emotional stress. The problem of controlling scientific inventions is not easy to solve, since the body of thought from which they are developed is held in uncritical esteem. It is a case of the parent being continually fearful of the might and power of its offspring.

Value-neutralism reflects the scepticism of modern society towards moral values, and numbs our responses to the many moral challenges that confront us. These include the prevention of global ecological disaster, the development of a world security force, the creation of a world federal government, and a host of other challenges that require a united moral resolve.

The philosophies that arise from an impersonal conception of science are power philosophies, where scientific technique is exempt from criticism and practically everything is regarded as raw material. Some measure of control over the applications of science can only be achieved by allowing for, indeed encouraging, the participation of the human spirit.

12. The Puritanical Mind

One can draw a parallel between positivist science and fundamentalist religion – both de-emphasize the role of the individual in their pursuit of objective truths. The puritanical Calvinists of the sixteenth and seventeenth centuries, for example, laid down a strict code of conduct and form of religious worship, aimed at impersonality. They sanctioned the wearing of only simple dress, outlawed the use of icons and decoration in churches, and followed a prescribed form of worship. Their scrupulous adherence to certain rites, laws of religious practice, and rules of observance is not unlike the positivist insistence on the scientific method proceeding along the lines of well-defined rules of logic and observation.

Just as the empiricist emphasizes the primary role of the senses, and what is measurable and observable, the puritanical Calvinist stressed the letter of Scripture, and specific codes of practice. Only the literal word was considered to be authoritative, and there was no room for personal interpretation or selection of religious verse. In the introduction to the 'Articles of Religion' issued in 1562, it was stressed that deviation from literal meaning was strictly prohibited:

No man hereafter shall either print or preach, to draw the Article aside in any way, but shall submit to it in the plain and full meaning thereof: and shall not put his own sense or comment to be the meaning of the Article, but shall take it in the literal and grammatical sense.[166]

The meaning of Scripture was held to be self-evident. For the positivist, the facts of science are conceived of in much the same way; they are seen as an infallible guide to the truth. Like the religious fundamentalist who denounces any attempt to draw wider meanings from Scripture, positivists shun all efforts to go beyond what the facts reveal.

Scripture, for the puritanical Calvinist, was believed to reveal objective and absolute truths for all time, up to the Day of Judgement. Individual believers were forced to surrender their identity and suppress their freedom of expression in favour of rigid rules and procedures. In fact the suppression of individual choice in Calvinism went so far that it led to the notion of limited atonement: that only those who were destined to be saved would be saved. In other words, it contained the notion of absolute determinism, with only the chosen few preordained to be saved. Salvation was not a matter of people choosing to believe or not to believe, but was predetermined; therefore, if we had foreknowledge of who was destined to be saved, we could predict the entire course of religious history. This is not dissimilar to the universal determinism of classical physics, as postulated by Laplace in the seventeenth century: his theory was that given knowledge of the state of the universe at any moment (the positions and velocities of all the particles in it, and so on), the state of the universe at a later time could be precisely predicted.[167] The mechanical universal determinism of Laplace had its moral equivalent in the Calvinist's conception of salvation, which in effect denied free will in terms of moral choice. The denial of free will in the intellectual sense is found in most modern models of human nature.

Positivists and religious fundamentalists also have much in common in their attempts to distinguish truth from falsehood. The verification test of the positivists is a means of distinguishing science from non-science, and it can be compared to the many articles of faith and practice which, for the fundamentalist in many religions, distinguishes the true believer from the unbeliever. Claims of exclusive truth put a ban on all forms of discourse other than those explicitly articulated by a certain ideology or creed. They inevitably result in a crusade aimed at purifying other people's beliefs and practices – in positivism, other philosophies were said to be nonsense, and for the Calvinist, other religions were evil. Applying simple tests to distinguish truth from falsehood requires a similar mentality to that involved in making black-and-white distinctions between good and evil. The chief characteristic of such a psychology is not unity, but division and fragmentation; not universality, but narrowness and exclusion; not what is believed, but what is rejected.

Strict empiricists and religious fundamentalists both employ a suspended form of logic, where their verification procedures, rules and methodology are applied to others, but not to themselves. This makes them self-righteous, concentrating on the evils and faults of others while completely oblivious to their own imperfections. Both these positions carry with them a suspicion of arrogance, where the individuality and freedom of others are denied, while leaving one's own self-knowledge or salvation unquestioned. The strict empiricist denies the self-knowledge of others while relying on his or her own self-knowledge, while the Calvinist denies salvation to others while being assured of his or her own route to salvation. Both show caprice and self-centredness.

These problems arise out of a notion that pure truth can be arrived at by using a clear-cut method and applying sweeping rules of reductionism and determinism. The individual experiences of either scientists or believers are ignored. Scientists are reduced to passive, mindless observers, performing a series of mechanical operations, and religion is reduced to a matter of blindly following rigid laws and observances, where the believer is expected simply to repeat passages of scriptural verse, or mechanically to perform rites and ceremonies. In neither case are legitimate mysteries acknowledged; all is in principle set out in advance, and truth is essentially a matter of following certain procedures.

We tend to have a short-sighted view of history, and are apt to forget that the corruption of religion is a recurrent phenomenon in human history; puritanical Calvinists were not the first adherents of religion to cling to literal conceptions about Scripture and law. When Christ admonished the Pharisees in the New Testament to 'stop judging by external standards and judge by true standards' (John 7:24), He was pointing to an archetypal occurrence in religious history: the spiritual vitality of its inner vision turning into blind adherence to external dogmas, rites, rules and laws. Religion reaches the point where the spirit of the law is forgotten, and the letter is scrupulously followed. Within the Jewish tradition itself, the limitation of 'judging by external standards' was clearly recognized: 'For man looketh on the outward appearance, but the Lord looketh on the heart' (I Samuel 16:7). The process of secularization is a very old one, and entails losing an inner experience and replacing it with external rules and laws, a psychological and spiritual state whose effects can be seen within both science and religion.

The familiar criticisms levelled against religious fundamentalists, that they use the letter of Scripture to provide simple black-and-white answers, use their faith as a means of avoiding uncertainties and complexities, rely on prescribed beliefs in order to avoid personal and moral responsibilities and the requirement of thinking independently – all these familiar accusations could also be applied to strict positivists. Abraham Maslow has noted that science conceived in impersonal terms is often used as a way of providing clear-cut certainties. He writes:

> Science, then, can be a defense. It can be primarily a safety philosophy, a security system, a complicated way of avoiding anxiety and upsetting problems. In the extreme instance it can be a way of avoiding life, a kind of self-cloistering. It can become – in the hands of some people, at least – a social institution with primarily defensive, conserving functions, ordering and stabilizing rather than discovering and renewing.[168]

As any scientist knows, it is easy to impress the non-scientist with a list of facts and figures that convey very little of what a scientific theory means, or where its significance lies. Moreover, the simple enumeration of facts often disguises a lack of understanding on the part of the scientist about his or her theory; the retreat into a list of facts may also be used as a psychological escape from the more difficult task of speaking on a personal level. There are many ways in which people use facts as a psychological crutch or as an avoidance mechanism. One has only to listen to rival politicians campaigning in an election to witness the abuse and manipulation of facts. A single politician might succeed in impressing on the public that his or her manifesto is supported by the 'facts', but after one has heard two rival politicians squabble on the eve of an election, one is left in no doubt that the 'facts' have been manipulated.

Often, scientists who stress the primary role of facts in discussions about their science do so in order to avoid the challenge of working together with other scientists, or to avoid a courageous leap of faith or a personal commitment to theories. If religion can be used as a psychological crutch, so can science. From this perspective, religious near-certainties do not differ from the near-certainties of positivism.

The dogmas of both religion and science are characterized by a common type of faith, which the psychologist Erich Fromm has called 'faith in the having mode'. This faith is impersonal, the roles of personal judgement and of uncertainty are minimized, and emphasis is placed on explicit rules and procedures. This type of faith demands little imagination or courage, and is based upon rejecting others. The religious zealot who condemns all faiths outside his own is just as spiritually impoverished as the scientist who denounces religion altogether as non-empirical or illogical. One of the few differences between the two is that the inter-religious feuds that result from fanaticism are easily identifiable, while the sceptical denouncements of positivist notions of science are not often understood to entail dogmatic psychology.

Scepticism about religion, which first developed out of important moral objections to religious hypocrisy raised by religious people themselves, now often involves the repetition of the same hackneyed accusations that appeared many decades ago. Such criticisms are often a matter of following the fashions of the day. Scepticism about religion is popularly associated with independence of mind, but can instead betray psychological insecurity. Conversely, strength of character is displayed by those who are able to commit themselves to beliefs contrary to prevailing fashions; this type of faith requires courage, imagination and personal involvement, and Erich Fromm has called it 'faith in the being mode'. Fromm makes the following distinction between these two types of faith:

> In a religious, political, or personal sense the concept of faith can have two entirely different meanings, depending upon whether it is used in the having mode, or in the being mode. Faith, in the having mode, is the possession of an answer for which one has no rational proof. It consists of formulations created by others, which one accepts because one submits to those others – usually a bureaucracy. It carries the feeling of certainty because of the real (or only imagined) power of the bureaucracy. It is the entry ticket to join a large group of people. It relieves one of the hard task of thinking for oneself and making decisions. . . . Faith in the having mode gives certainty; it claims to pronounce ultimate, unshakable knowledge . . . faith in the having mode, is a crutch for those who want to be certain. . . . In the being mode, faith is an entirely different phenomenon. Can we live without faith? Must not the nursling have faith in its mother's breast? Must we all not have faith in other beings, in those whom we love, and in ourselves? . . . it is a certainty of a truth that cannot be proven by rationally compelling evidence, yet truth I am certain of because of my experiential, subjective evidence.[169]

Faith in the being mode is experienced personally, while faith in the having mode is possessed as one possesses an object, in an impersonal sense. Both science and religion can be treated in these two different ways. Science in the having mode becomes mere spectator science, the mechanical act of listing facts, observations and figures. Religion in the having mode is the blind following of rules and rites. Strict empiricism and literalist religion both emphasize externals – everything external to oneself. Both science and religion can be believed in the having mode, for reasons, say, of achieving social acceptance. By contrast, in the being mode, both science and religion have a genuine spiritual foundation. They consist of courageous leaps of faith and imagination; they are a personal journey discovering deeper and deeper layers of meaning.

Science is founded on respect, love, wonder and a commitment to finding truth and meaning. Although they are crucial to all significant science, these values cannot be measured or weighed by scientific instruments; they exist only as an inner human experience. For all our modern progress, our understanding of the special characteristics that define our humanity has remained essentially the same, and knowledge of the external world cannot be used as substitute for knowing oneself, or understanding moral responsibilities.

In this century, an underlying concern behind most attempts to describe human nature has been that the human self-portrait should remain firmly within the realm of our human experience. Many of the criticisms directed against traditional religion have been made with this principle in mind. Secularism has typically taken the form of a rebellion against religion on the grounds that traditional religion limited human freedom and creativity. It was accused of having exclusively 'otherworldly' concerns, and therefore neglecting the human world. But does a religious description of human nature intrinsically involve us in going beyond our experience? This is the question to which we next turn our attention.

13. The Experience of God

••

While it might be accepted that science and religion have many features in common, it is clear that they also differ in fundamental ways. Religion is founded on the authority of revelation, while science seems to proceed without an explicit appeal to such an authority. Religion invariably involves the concept of a divine, omniscient, omnipresent being, or the concept of an immortal soul that survives death, which a positivist would regard as magical and nonsensical ideas, and dismiss on the grounds that they relate to matters far outside our experience. Typical challenges to followers of religion are to 'prove God exists', 'prove that a human soul exists', 'prove that there is an after-life', and so on. Others ask 'is the concept of God falsifiable?', or 'is the concept of God rationally coherent?'

Innumerable books have been written asking and answering such questions over hundreds of years. Yet a characteristic ambiguity surrounds them. Take, for example, the question of the existence of God. The concept of God encompasses many notions, including God in nature (pantheism), God in terms of spirits (supernatural experiences), God in Christ (the Christian incarnation), the God of the philosophers (deism), God the Law-Giver (Jehovah and Allah), and so on. Moreover, there seem to be as many different definitions of God as there are people who believe in God. This diversity in understanding the concept of God is not in itself a problem – in fact all these different conceptions of God can be thought of as complementary in nature: each one teaches us more about the attributes of God. The Bahá'í Faith, a religion founded in the middle of the last century, regards the different approaches to God within the world's major spiritual traditions as equally valid. If they are taken together, our concept of God is greatly enriched. In the Bahá'í writings, the founders of the world's major religions are described as successive 'luminaries', as 'Temples of the Cause of God, Who have appeared clothed in divers attire'.[170] Yet it is this flexibility in the understanding of God that creates the perceived clash with modern science.

The confusion over the vagueness of concepts such as God is related to the way one's questions are formulated. The modern approach is usually to adopt some empirical or positivist approach, where the concept of God is primarily formulated in external terms. When religious people are asked to 'prove God exists', even if the individual who poses the question is not consciously aware of it, he or she is often referring to the kinds of proofs thought to exist in scientific investigation.

The notion that science proves theories to be true is a naive conception of science: a finite number of observations can never establish the certainty of a theory, and there will always be a residual leap of faith involved in 'proving' the theory to be true. Thus, the first point to bear in mind about someone who challenges the religious believer to 'prove God exists' is that he or she is expecting the proof to accord with an empiricist's definition of science, where theories are thought to be definitively proved by empirical facts.

Secondly, the question also tacitly relies on the modern positivist and empirical notion of giving priority to acts of quantitative measurement and objective observation, where the universe is regarded as being composed of a collection of inanimate objects. The question of God existing will be assessed in these positivist terms, and a verification test of some kind is usually implicit. The individual who formulates such a challenge may never have read Hume's philosophy, or even heard of logical positivism and its subsequent failure as a philosophy of science, yet his or her argument against the existence of God often bears close resemblance to an application of the positivist's verification test, or Hume's Fork.

Sometimes the challenger has read a little philosophy (perhaps from Karl Popper) and might formulate the challenge as: 'is the concept of God falsifiable?', in the belief that he or she has succeeded in avoiding the problems of scientific induction by requiring not direct proof, but falsification. But this is still equivalent to applying a positivist verification test, which suffers from many well-known problems. There are very few concepts even in science that are directly falsifiable, and Popper himself did not use the falsifiability criterion in this way. He used it as a way of distinguishing between pseudo-science and real science — and demonstrated that Marxism and Freud's psychoanalysis was 'unscientific'.[171]

Ironically, much of Popper's philosophy was directed against logical positivism, and was concerned with establishing human 'freedom and creativity' — he describes the world of the mind as an 'open universe'.[172] Referring to the founders of logical positivism, Popper wrote: 'It was clear to me that all these people were looking for a criterion of demarcation not so much between science and pseudoscience as between science and metaphysics . . . any such criterion was bound to lead to trouble, since metaphysical ideas are often the forerunners of scientific ones.'[173] Popper was well aware that the more fundamental the concept, such as the notion of truth, belief in causality, the existence of the external world, and so on, the more difficult it is to falsify.

The empirical world view, which lies behind denials that God exists, tacitly assumes that God would be an object like any other in the universe, and could be measured, observed and quantified by normal empirical methods. In this sense, the empirical world-view assumes the universe to be closed. It bears obvious similarities to the medieval closed universe, which envisaged a finite set of hierarchical rings, sealed above by the sphere of heaven and below by hell. The empirical universe is closed to everything beyond quantitative measurement. Its self-imposed ceiling is more subtle than the medieval one, but exists nevertheless.

Central to the modern walled-in idea of the universe is the rejection of mystery. By reducing the entire cosmos to objects of measurement and observation, the modern mind protects itself from the unknown, under the mistaken notion that it has captured the spirit of scientific investigation. It has not. Leaving out the spiritual foundations of science grossly misrepresents it.

The world of God is by definition infinitely higher than the human world, so to base an understanding of God on human empirical notions would be like demanding that an ant crawling across a concert-hall floor name the piece of music the orchestra is playing. The empirical approach to the notion of God can only describe God in terms of object-like qualities, and the same is true of studying human nature in such terms. Purely empirical methods taken by themselves reduce the world to a meaningless jumble of object-perceptions.

It is characteristic of the modern mind to attach primary importance to outward appearances. As western society became more secular in its vision, the fundamentals of religion were increasingly cast in external terms, and the approach to the concept of God came to be more and more in terms of God as an object. Medieval people had felt the presence of God always near at hand; the works of God were seen to operate in daily life, both in society and in the soul. The existence of God was perceived as a perfectly natural fact, rather like the sun rising every day. But as Christianity fragmented, God became increasingly remote from the everyday lives of believers. In seventeenth-century Calvinism, God was primarily conceived of as law-giver and judge, sending down punishments to those who were led astray. The idea of God was modelled on a stern father figure, sitting upon the clouds and passing harsh judgements on sinners. There arose a tendency to place great emphasis on the formal characteristics of God, as for instance the First Cause, the grand designer of the universe. In medieval times God was also the Final Cause, towards which all creation was constantly moving, not just a First Cause who wound up the universe like a clock and then let it tick on, interfering no more with it.

Over the past few centuries, the physical existence of God has become the crucial question for believers and non-believers alike, whereas previously the spiritual attributes of God were considered to be more important, especially the relationship of God to humanity. As religion was sapped of its unifying inner vitality, the concept of God was approached in more and more external terms.

If we insist on judging in purely external terms, we will also be limited by them. We will have covered our inner ears and eyes, and closed our minds and hearts to spiritual meanings. To be closed to the concept of God on empiricist grounds is to live one's spiritual life in a cocoon of pseudo-science. Religion, like science, is founded on an inner spiritual experience, and the nature of God is an inseparable part of this experience. The majority of those who believe in God do not do so out of the compelling logic of the philosophical arguments found in deism. Nor is belief in God founded on a convincing performance of various rites and rituals.

The major inspiration for belief in God has come from the founders of religion. In religious cosmology, the founders of religion are like suns; they are the source of spiritual life for their followers. The founder of a religion, such as Moses, Christ or Muhammad, is a spiritual link with God and provides the main source of belief in God's existence (similar founders are assumed to have appeared throughout humanity's history). It is primarily in response to the appearance of such 'suns' that the notion of God has flourished in the hearts and minds of people. Without this inner growth, the universe within, to use Platonic language, would be a spiritually barren wilderness, with only confused shadows of the external world.

Religion in its pure form, shorn of dogmas, superstitions, fixed rites and practices, is an indwelling spiritual experience, and a fundamental experience of human nature. The founders of religion are somehow able to foster the growth of spiritual fruit in the hearts and minds of their followers; to bring out heroic acts of faith; to provide a universe of inner meanings and truths; to inspire bonds of love; to heighten a sense of justice and compassion – all this and much more emanates from a personal spiritual experience. Religion touches the core of human nature, and reaches the most noble part of us. Human nature can be thought of as composed of many layers of different selves, and religion penetrates beyond the animal self, beyond the conditioned self, beyond the robotic self, beyond all possibilities of external observation, to an ineffable spiritual core – to God within.

The human experience of an inner light of spiritual consciousness lies at the foundation of all the world's major spiritual traditions. Knowledge of God is kindled in human hearts, and intensified by the founders of religions; it is as if they unlock the spiritual potential latent in humanity. Human nature might be likened to a candle (an analogy used in the Bahá'í writings[174]), which has the potential to give out spiritual light, but can only be kindled by the rays of the invisible spiritual suns that light up the sky of religious cosmology. No external approach can compare with this inner approach to God.

Descriptions of God as all-powerful, as universal creator and so on are poor substitutes for this inner spiritual experience of understanding God. All attributes of God are described in terms of the physical universe, or more precisely in terms of what the physical universe is not. Yet since the world of God is infinitely higher than the human world, description of God in such terms will always be extremely limited.

The inward character of religious experience is subtle. On one level, the words and life of the founder of a religion can be evaluated in object-terms. If we observe an object such as a stone, the visual qualities of the stone, its colour, size, orientation and so on, are conveyed to us by reflection of the incident light falling on it, say from the sun. A certain amount of this incident light is absorbed by the stone, and the reflected light conveys information about it to the observer. The absorption of different frequencies of light in the object enables the observer to detect colour information, and so on. The observer does not interact with the object, but merely detects reflected light. The eye of the observer is directed outwards, and his or her identity, beliefs and so on do not seem to be relevant to the observation. Religion might, on one level, be studied in a similar way. Religious experience for some may be equated with absorbing information in terms of statements about the origin of the universe, teachings about God, an afterlife, a set of laws, ethics and codes to follow. This is a common way of approaching religion today, but it is a one-dimensional approach that does little to capture the depth of religious experience.

The teachings that make up a religion are not 'observed', in the impersonal object-terms just described, by genuine followers of that religion. The way in which they regard their founder is more like looking at a perfectly polished mirror than at a stone. In a perfectly polished mirror, one not only captures the image of the sun, its relative position in the sky, the surrounding landscape and so on, but one sees an undistorted self-image: the observer can observe himself or herself. Religious experience is a process of self-illumination, self-examination and self-discovery. In a perfectly polished mirror, none of the mirror's characteristics are perceived by the observer. He or she may set out to examine the mirror as one would study a stone, expecting to find its visual form in its reflected light, but in fact the reflection represents the observer's own image.

In this analogy of the mirror, observer and landscape, the sun might represent God, who illuminates everything; the perfectly polished mirror is a founder of religion; and the surrounding landscape is the world external to our minds. Everything in the landscape reflects, to its own degree, the light of the sun. The uniqueness of the founders of religion lies in the fact that they mirror the sun's light perfectly – to a degree not found elsewhere. This analogy is taken directly from the Bahá'í writings.[175]

Spiritual enlightenment is not a matter of following the dictates of something external to the observer, since it is primarily the observer's own identity that is mirrored back to him or her. The notion of religious experience being based upon an authority external to oneself is misleading – looking up to a higher authority involves a search within oneself. The humbling process of looking towards the founder of a religion for guidance involves people in discovering more about themselves, because religion is about releasing the spiritual potential latent within human nature. The goal of religious experience can be understood in terms of becoming more like a perfectly polished mirror, moving towards a state of selflessness, and reflecting to a greater degree the light of God. The founder of a religion is our route to finding God, mirroring the attributes of God to us, which are none other than the attributes of God lying within us.

Although notions of approaching God in purely physical terms, including the concept of God as the First Cause, are useful in making us open-minded, they are of limited use in conveying the spiritual attributes of God. Deist arguments do not prove the existence of God, but they do indicate that the explanation for our world is more likely to come from outside it than from within it. This should make us more open to the possibility of the existence of higher worlds beyond our own, but it does not prove their existence.

The design argument seeks to prove God's existence by likening the order found in nature to a human artefact such as a watch. The argument states that like a watch, the universe was designed and made for a purpose – nature is a testimony to God's handiwork. Isaac Newton conceived a design argument based upon the simplicity and unity of the laws of nature. This finds direct support in the world's religious scriptures, but can it be considered proof of God's existence? Many refutations by philosophers such as Kant, Hume and Russell claimed to have invalidated the design argument for God's existence on the grounds that it goes beyond our experience. Our experience of human design and purpose, they argued, cannot be extrapolated to apply on the universal level. Yet such objections could also be made against any theory in science since, in a strict empiricist sense, every scientific theory goes beyond our experience except tautological ones like '0=0'. The problem hinges once again upon the notion of proof.

The design argument for God's existence cannot be expected to provide absolute certainty, and is only plausible when compared to the view that the universe is a random, purposeless collection of objects bearing no connection with one another. Most people have believed in the design argument in the sense that an underlying design to the universe is much more likely than a background chaos. Newton contrasted the orderly motion of the planets with the erratic motion of comets in formulating his version of the argument. Ancient philosophers such as Plato and Aristotle formulated versions of it, as did many medieval scholastic philosophers in Islam, Judaism and Christianity, such as Avicenna, Maimonides and Aquinas. The seventeenth-century scientists believed in it, and there are even some modern versions such as the 'anthropic principle' of the mid-1980s, which was based upon the observation that life on earth depends on the extraordinary precision of universal constants in nature, and if they differed even fractionally from their present values the conditions necessary to sustain life on earth would not have existed. This has been said to provide evidence that somehow the laws of physics are 'designed' to create life on earth.

Design arguments for God's existence have had remarkable universal appeal throughout history, and scientists in particular have found them persuasive. But most of their advocates do not intend to provide definitive proofs for God's existence, although the validity of science itself relies on faith in one or other version of the design argument and the findings of science are continually reinforcing it. Through every discovery of science, nature appears in greater unity and order, and it is difficult to separate this from the notion of design.

The power of the design argument does not lie in providing us with proof about God, but in articulating the deep sentiment, universally felt, that there must be more to this world than one can explain from within it. It relies on a faith in the rationality of the laws in nature, and hence is intrinsic to the spiritual foundations of science.

These conclusions also apply to the cosmological argument for God's existence. This starts by assuming that all things are preceded by a cause, and postulates that God is the First Cause anchoring the chain of all causes in the universe, which is itself uncaused. The cosmological argument, like the design argument, has a long history associated with it, and has also found universal appeal. But again, it does not definitively prove anything, and its power lies in the fact that it is a universal generalization of something that is very much part of our experience: that everything seems to be preceded by a cause. The plausibility of the argument is shown by comparing it to the notion of the universe being without a cause, that it is simply a brute fact. Whatever the advocates for a causeless universe may say, very few people have found this to be plausible. Why should we suspend the idea of causation at the universal level when it is so much a part of our experience on all other levels? This is particularly true of our scientific experience, where success in science is founded on a search for the underlying causes of phenomena, and faith in the causation principle. The successes of modern science affirm our belief in causation rather than weaken it, but it cannot be definitively validated, and one can always be sceptical about it.

It might be objected that the cosmological argument forces us to give up the notion of causation at some point, since the First

Cause is itself uncaused, and hence it does not accord with our experience. But the spirit underlying the notion of the First Cause, which is not contained in the cosmological argument itself, is the intuition of an ultimate cause with some rationale. This is to be contrasted with the notion of a universe based on irrational causes, that is, to say governed by blind physical forces. Thus suspension of the idea of causation on the level of the First Cause is quite different to its suspension on the physical level.

The discoveries of science are constantly strengthening the plausibility of the cosmological and design arguments – not by proving the existence of God, but by showing that the correct explanation of the universe is more likely to come from outside it than from within it.[176] Every scientific advance confirms our faith in the universal validity of the principle of causation. As science uncovers deeper and deeper connections in the universe, revealing greater layers of unity throughout the cosmos and describing the laws of nature in more profound terms, the mystery behind these laws deepens. As a chain of deeper and deeper causes operating throughout the universe is uncovered, the intuition of a First Cause is strengthened.

A simple example can be given to illustrate these points. Bertrand Russell, in a radio debate with the philosopher and theologian Frederick Copleston about the existence of God, refused to make the inductive leap about the universe having a cause, going so far as to state that the term 'universe', although useful, was in fact meaningless. Generalizing from individual causes to a cause which applied to the universe as a whole, he said, was similar to saying that since each human being has a mother, the human race has a mother. Russell argued that since such a generalization is not valid, the cosmological argument for the existence of God is not tenable.[177] Yet the progress of science has weakened Russell's objection. Today, when we speak of the universe as a single entity, we do so in a scientifically correct way. The Big Bang theory shows us that the universe has a common origin, and that prior causes acted upon the universe as a whole.

Russell missed the spirit of the argument. There is much even within science that can only be described in the language of parables. The Big Bang is often described as the birth of our universe.[178] It is quite likely that there are many Big Bangs, and that our known universe is only a small part of a much greater universe, so the leap to causation on a universal level is still an infinitely large one. And yet, the more science progresses, the wider the circle of causes seem to have become. Each newly discovered cause in science seems to be more profound than existing ones – more universal, bringing our vision of the universe into a greater unity. The concept of a single First Cause lying behind all these causes is a perfectly natural one, consistent with our scientific experience.

The discoveries of science should serve to make us more open-minded to ultimate causes and to an ultimate design in the universe, not closed to them. Despite all the positivist rhetoric about science only answering 'how' questions, scientific investigation is ultimately grounded in 'why' questions, and aims to solve cosmological mysteries. The goal of a unified field theory in modern physics aims to arrive at a single law of nature for the universe. It is based on the vision that there is a single comprehensible explanation behind all that we see and experience. In this sense, the spiritual intuitions driving modern science are no different from those of ancient or medieval science. Science is founded upon successful generalizations of our experience to the universal level. The kinds of intuitions that make the cosmological and design arguments for God's existence plausible also make scientific investigation meaningful.

Belief in God is better understood in terms of our spiritual experience, rather than the supposed virtues or defects of empirical observations and rational arguments. The corruption of religion, leading to religious fragmentation, has been the prime reason for the weakening of belief in God ever since the Middle Ages. The effect of religious corruption might be likened to the arrival of clouds on the spiritual horizon (an analogy also taken from the Bahá'í writings[179]), having the effect of blocking out the rays of the spiritual sun on which the religion is founded. The inner life of religious followers will be sapped of energy, and the link to the spiritual sun becomes obscured and confused. Under these conditions, religions fragment, and their followers lose sight of the deeper meanings of their faith. In these twilight times, conflicts

and misunderstandings multiply as the religious landscape is filled
with ghostly, unrelated shadows creeping across what was once a
clear and unified landscape. What were indisputable facts of inner
experience begin to require rational proofs and external
corroboration.

While the inner spiritual life of a society is strong, the truths of
religion are regarded as objective. Such a society will find that the
existence of God and a universal moral order are objective facts
because they represent spiritual experiences shared by the majority
of its members. For most societies that have existed throughout
history, the existence of God has been affirmed in this way. But in
the twilight periods of religious belief, where corruption dominates
a society's experience of religion, the depth of spiritual experience
is lost, and religion appears in superficial external terms. Spiritual
matters start to become fragmented into differing, incompatible
beliefs, and the clarity of the religious landscape is lost. The
spiritual landscape may become so darkened that the very
existence of the universe within may be doubted. Everything that
was formerly lit up by spiritual light, belief in God, in a universal
moral order, in the sacredness of the earth, in the spiritual nature
of humanity – will be darkened by doubt, and such truths will no
longer be facts of our experience.

Such a state of mind seems to be the cause of the spiritual
confusion of modern times. The modern mind, wandering through
a spiritually darkened landscape, stumbles on conflicting fragments
of human nature, characterized by inherent inconsistencies and
suspended forms of logic.

The concept of God cannot be successfully analysed in an
impersonal way, any more than is possible for the nature of science.
Our knowledge of God is dependent on our experience of those
who come in God's name, and the light of inner experience.

14. The Spiritual Instinct

•••

Just as the external universe extends far beyond our vision, the universe of human nature extends far beyond our rational comprehension. What appears to be an empty patch in the night sky in fact contains worlds upon worlds, galaxies of stars within galaxies of stars; and our rational thoughts contain deeper and deeper layers of feelings, intuitions and instincts.

The mind is most popularly described today as a passive, ghostly reflection of the external world, an epiphenomenon arising out of natural processes. Ironically, Descartes' philosophy is often cited as influential in contributing to this view, but this thesis relies on a superficial account of Descartes' philosophy. Descartes journeyed deeper and deeper into his own mind in a search to find truth. Modern investigations are typically aimed in the opposite direction, where they point to objects further and further away from the mind.

At the very beginning of his search, Descartes discounted sense information as a reliable foundation for knowledge – precisely the opposite of today's empiricist attitude. For Descartes, empiricism only described the world in superficial terms; it was the very surface layer of knowledge. He recognized that empirical knowledge on its own could be very misleading, like the distorted appearance of a straight stick partially immersed in water. For Descartes, the empirical approach only provided a starting point in the search for knowledge.

Descartes also found that he could doubt the validity of mathematics. Even the apparently measurable qualities of the world, the ones Descartes is commonly supposed to have considered as primary in relation to mental qualities, he discounted as a method of acquiring certain knowledge. The certainty positivism assigns to mathematical knowledge is, according to Descartes' philosophy, misplaced. He understood that mathematical reasoning, like sense perceptions, could ultimately be illusory. Two plus two can equal five, if we really want it to.

Even the existence of the external world could be doubted. Descartes found that there was, in principle, no way of distinguishing between a dreamful state and a conscious one. What he took to be a conscious state might actually turn out to be a dream. The reality of the external world was not an indisputable, proven fact.

Descartes' search ended in his affirmation of the power of the mind above all else: he found that while he could doubt everything, he could not doubt that he was thinking, since this doubt also involved thought. 'I think, therefore I am.' This conclusion stands in direct contradiction to today's prevailing conception of human knowledge, which rests on the primacy of empirical and mathematical methods and of the external world over the knowledge of our minds.

Descartes found the irreducibility of human thought to be a sign of certainty. His philosophical search amounted to discovering different layers of truth within himself; the empirical level of truth only lay at the surface, the mathematical layer provided a deeper layer of truth, and so on, while the most fundamental truth lay in the irreducible power of human thought. A notion of truth, a search after truth, leaps of faith, acts of open-mindedness, an ability to reason – these are all irreducible facets of human nature, inextricably linked to the thinking process. Thus, Descartes' conclusion might also be put in the following form: I have a notion of truth and meaning, I respect truth and meaning, I search for truth and meaning, I strive to be open-minded, I perform acts of faith, I believe in the unity and rationality of nature and the ability of human minds to understand it, I am able to reason – therefore I am. The fundamental core of human nature is thus spiritual, non-rational and non-empirical. Human nature is composed of many layers of selves, but the most characteristic feature of humanity is the spiritual self.

All noble enterprises, science, religion, art and ethics, rely on the spiritual core of human nature prevailing over the influence of other superficial selves. While Descartes' search for indubitable truths in effect reached the conclusion that the spiritual self is more fundamental to human character than any other self, it was not new. All the world's spiritual traditions reach the same conclusion. All religions, for instance, are based upon a belief in the primacy of the spiritual over the material in human nature.

There has been no convincing refutation of Descartes' conclusion that the spiritual mind is more fundamental and more powerful than the empirical or mathematical layers of the self. No theories in science have led us to doubt this. Quite the opposite is true: the success of science itself is one of the clearest demonstrations of the power of the mind over the material. The power of thought is still the experience upon which all our knowledge is founded. Modern attempts to deny the primacy of the spiritual in human nature, such as behaviourism and robotomorphism, involve themselves in a welter of internal inconsistencies, amounting in one way or another to self-defeat. Modern models of human nature that merely dismiss the spiritual dimension from the outset capture very little of our experience of being human. Their methods of enquiry are quite different to the one Descartes used, or the ones enjoined upon us in any of the world's spiritual traditions. Descartes' discovery came from inward meditation. Modern approaches to understanding human nature are directed away from the mind, to a plethora of external observations and measurements. This is a matter of misplaced emphasis: our spirit of exploration and discovery in the external universe is not matched by a corresponding spirit for the inner universe. We are more comfortable conquering far away moons than exploring inner space.

What of the modern philosophical objections to Descartes' so-called dualism? Most modern books on the philosophy of mind start with a short dismissal of 'dualism', that is, of the idea that the mind is made up of a composite mixture of spiritual and material elements.[180] Some of the arguments usually levied against a spiritual-material mind include the objection that a mind-spirit resists normal scientific research techniques; that a mind-spirit

cannot be located physically; the difficulty of deciding at what
point in a human embryo's growth it acquires a mind-spirit (or at
what point in human evolution our species acquired minds); and
that a mind-spirit does not obey the conservation of energy
principle. Most of these objections are not as problematic as they
are taken to be, and most are characterized by an implicit
assumption that the mind can be adequately described in external,
empirical terms, based on an impersonal conception of science.

Take, for instance, the objection that normal methods of
scientific research cannot be used on a mind-spirit. The obvious
response here is that such a limitation does not detract in any way
from the mind's spiritual nature. Indeed, such an objection fails to
assess the fundamental nature of the mind. It cannot be treated
like any other object, weighed, measured, observed or dissected,
since it is the very entity through which all scientific research is
made possible. One cannot be objective about it, just as in the
same way that one cannot examine a telescope while looking
through it. The mind is composed of the irreducible elements upon
which science is founded – such as the notion of truth, faith in the
rationality of nature and our ability to understand it – and all
attempts at studying truth, faith and rationality will inevitably
employ them. The more fundamental the question, the less
objective we can be about it. We are also unable to investigate the
law of causality or the existence of the external world by using the
normal methods of science, but this does not preclude us from
believing in them. The fact that the spiritual nature of the mind
resists normal methods of scientific research shows it to be a
fundamental cosmological mystery.

The problems of physically locating the mind-spirit are also
unimportant to an understanding of the character of the mind.
There is no compelling reason why the mind-spirit should have a
physical location. If the mind-spirit is located outside space–time,
there is of course the question of how it interacts with the brain.
There can be no simple answer to this, since every attempted
explanation will inevitably employ concepts formulated from
within space–time. Thus every analogy describing the relationship
of the mind to the body must be strictly incorrect. The mind and
body are two fundamentally distinct categories, and a true

understanding of the mind is unlikely to be possible. The mind can be likened to a higher world incarnate in our brains, and we will thus always be limited in describing it, since it is precisely the spiritual dimension of the mind that lies behind all our explanations.

The problem of precisely when a mind comes into existence during the growth of a human embryo, or when souls came into existence in human evolution, is also a profound mystery. From the moment of conception of a human foetus, a specific personality seems to be created. The spiritual dimension to the human mind, in the case of both the individual and the race, seems to grow progressively stronger from its initial inception. There is no fundamental philosophical difficulty in either case. The human mind-spirit may be likened to the fruit of a tree. If one asks when the fruit comes into existence, the answer would be that the existence of the fruit is always potential in the seed from the moment the seed is planted in the ground, although it only reveals itself gradually during the growth of the tree. Likewise, the qualities of the human soul only gradually appear in the growth of a human being, and only progressively appeared in our collective evolution, although in either case they may have existed from the very beginning. This analogy should not be taken too literally, since all attempts at understanding the soul in empirical and rational terms will be invalid. The general point here is that there cannot be any fundamental philosophical objection to the existence of the spiritual nature of human beings based upon not knowing precisely when a soul comes into existence.

It should also perhaps be pointed out that belief in a mind-spirit starting its life at the moment of conception does not necessarily imply that an immortal entity is somehow created by an event located in time. We are not required to believe that a certain type of physical event can create immortality. What it does entail, however, is recognizing that an immortal entity becomes imprinted with a specific identity – at the moment of conception.

If the notion of something being immortal seems strange to us, we must not forget that the particles that make up our own bodies, and indeed the entire universe, are also understood to be immortal. The fundamental particles of modern physics – electrons, quarks, and so on – are thought to be indivisible, and hence immortal. At present, the evolution of the universe from the moment of the Big Bang is explained in terms of the combination and recombination of these fundamental particles. The earth, vegetation, animals and human beings use largely the same store of fundamental particles for their existence. Since there are so many of them, there is a significant probability that some of these 'immortal' entities that are presently within the reader, or within the author, were also to be found in the bodies of Einstein, Newton, Descartes, Plato and Aristotle! Perhaps immortality is not such a strange phenomenon after all, but one that can be found close to hand, too close for us to really appreciate.

An individual soul can be likened to our universe. Just as the universe is thought to have had its beginning at the moment of the Big Bang, so an individual soul might be understood to have a definite birth at the moment of conception. Just as our universe has been expanding, the inner universe of a soul is constantly growing. The inner cosmos, like the outer one, goes through many phases in its evolution. Connections in the mind rapidly multiply in early infancy, just as the most important developments in the physical universe occurred in its first few minutes.[181] Gradually, in both cases, a unique identity emerges. Both are immortal but also have a definite beginning: the 'birth' of the universe involves bringing together and reorganizing pre-existing fundamental particles, while the creation of the soul involves imprinting eternal spirit with a unique identity and character.

The objection that the soul does not obey laws of energy conservation is not tenable. One cannot apply physical constraints to non-physical entities. One cannot expect the soul to obey the same laws of physics as physical objects. In any case, anyone familiar with the properties of a magnetic field knows that an electron can be deflected by it, and still retain the same kinetic energy it had when entering it. Although the magnetic field deflected the electron, as far as the electron is concerned energy is conserved.

The analogy of the mind emerging from the brain like a fruit from a tree, and the notion that the specific identity of an immortal soul comes into being at the moment of conception, come directly from the Bahá'í writings.[182] Such analogies are generally representative of the many other descriptions of the soul in the world's spiritual traditions. They illustrate the intuition that although the mind appears to be contingent upon the body, it is something more; it has a certain independence from the body and does not come to an end when the constituent parts to our bodies disperse.

Another analogy given in the Bahá'í writings, which is also echoed in many of the world's spiritual traditions, is the image of the soul's existence in this physical world being like that of a bird imprisoned in a cage. When the cage is opened, or taken away, or destroyed, the bird is free to fly upwards on its spiritual journey.[183] Yet another analogy for the connection of the soul to the body is that it is like light falling on a mirror: the light may be likened to 'waves' of the soul, which are reflected in the operations of the brain.[184] The light of the soul remains unaffected if the mirror is broken.

John Hatcher, discussing the Bahá'í writings about the soul, compares the connection between the soul and the brain to the way information is broadcast from a television transmitter and detected by a television receiver.[185] The waves of electromagnetic energy traversing the earth's atmosphere, reflected around the world, are independent of the television receiver. It is only by tuning our television sets to the correct frequency, by decoding information in a certain way, that we can view the images formed on our television screens. Similarly, the 'thought waves' of the soul might traverse an 'inner space' and be detected by the brain, which is in some sense 'tuned' to receive them. Malfunctions in the television set do not affect the transmitted signals; a blurred image on our television sets, as most of us are well aware, is often due to a faulty set and does not indicate a problem with the transmitted signals. Likewise, if the soul may be thought of as 'transmitting' information to the brain, it is only in its 'reception' that the soul will appear to be affected by the state of the brain.

Like all other analogies, this modern metaphor must not be interpreted too literally. For example, experience in this world helps to strengthen the soul, and gives it impetus to move along a spiritual path; this is not captured in the television-transmitter analogy. The analogies found in the writings of the world's spiritual traditions are more accurate, like the comparison between the condition of the soul in this world and that of a foetus in the womb of the mother, given frequently in the Bahá'í writings.[186] This analogy captures the idea of the soul evolving, which is intrinsic to the religious understanding of the soul. The human condition on earth is one of preparation: just as a foetus develops faculties to use in this world, a religious conception of the soul understands it is preparing for a 'birth' in another world. Our purpose in this world is to develop qualities of the soul, such as justice, honesty, humility, love, peace, wisdom and understanding, in preparation for another step along our path towards God. Inherent in a religious vision of the soul is the notion of its progress towards becoming more God-like.

All our images of the soul must, however, be extremely limited because we can only glimpse the spiritual nature of the soul, or sense its progress on an inner journey. We cannot give a full account of it, just as a foetus in the womb of its mother is unable to understand the true purpose of its immediate environment. In this sense, the spiritual nature of the soul is perhaps better understood in terms of an instinct – a sign of something much deeper within us. The fact that in every part of the world, at all periods throughout our history, human beings have described their spiritual experience in terms of an inner journey, have seen this physical life as a passage to something much greater, have believed in a God and in an ultimate rationale to all that we experience – all this leads one to conclude that the spiritual nature of human beings is something that can only be understood on the instinctual level. The spiritual nature of human beings is something that has first and foremost to be experienced, but it is an intuition that has been greatly strengthened by the world's major religious traditions.

The historian Arnold Toynbee refers to this religious side of human beings as a 'distinctive spiritual ingredient of human nature'.[187] Instincts are usually there for a purpose, and if there are aspects to human behaviour that can be interpreted in terms of a survival instinct, then there are other sides to human nature, all the nobler ones, which can be explained in terms of a spiritual instinct. Our drive to be creative and to acquire meaning is part of the spiritual instinct that is ultimately rooted in our search for God.

The problems with modern philosophy's attempts to analyse the nature of the mind stem from adopting the positivist approach of describing the mind in external, measurable terms. The result filters out all spiritual characteristics of the mind and reduces it to something it is not. This is like reducing a temple to a pile of bricks and then weighing each brick in turn, to discover the blueprint from which the temple was constructed.

Consider the brain-identity theory of the mind, which achieved considerable popularity in the 1950s. This theory states that every mental event stems from a prior neurophysiological event, that is, mental events are based on chemical reactions. Yet by insisting that mental events be explicable in terms of physical ones, the theory suffers from many philosophical inconsistencies that have now been well-recognized. One problem is that physical events are of a fundamentally different category to mental events: the physical events in the brain are presumably finite in number, whereas mental events seem to be infinite. What would be the physical event corresponding to the concept of 'chairs' or of infinity or zero, and how would it differ from the event behind the intention 'I want to do some shopping today'? There is no way of achieving the one-to-one correspondence of physical events to mental events demanded by the brain-identity theory. It also appears that far from it being the case that mental events are dependent on physical events, the reverse often seems to be true. If, for instance, I decide to raise my arm, the cause of this physical event originated in a purposeful mental intention. There is no reason to assume that brain events are more fundamental to human behaviour than mental events.

Most modern theories of the mind postulate that mental events are in some way an epiphenomenon or by-product of physical processes. This is true of the brain-identity theorists, the behaviourists, and the many robotomorphic models of human behaviour. All such philosophies of mind are ultimately self-defeating: if the thoughts of human beings are merely the by-product of physical processes, then the theory of epiphenomenalism itself will be the by-product of a physical process. This robs it of any meaning content: to understand the argument, one would need to examine the physical process that gave rise to it, rather than the truth or falsehood of any mental form of reasoning. The epiphenomenalist theory cannot account for itself, since if it were true, the theory itself will be an unimportant by-product of a physical process.

A simple analogy can be drawn here to illustrate the point further. Imagine the mind were comparable to a steam engine, say a locomotive, where the driving force comes from a specific physical process, such as in this case the burning of coal. The epiphenomenalist position might be said to identify human thoughts with the steam puffing out of the locomotive, in the belief that our thoughts are essentially by-products of a physical process. If this is so, when epiphenomenalists put forward their views, we are confronted with something comparable to hot air! There is a contradiction in the epiphenomenalists' position, since they would want to say that the argument amounts to something much more than hot air. The problem with the epiphenomenalists' position is that they have omitted to take themselves into account in their theory of the human mind. We cannot be objective or impersonal about our thinking. This is precisely why Descartes' 'I think, therefore I am' needs to be restated.

Although the modern approach to the mind is generally a reductionist one, opposition to it is growing. In particular, the habitual debunking of humanity and its place in the cosmos in the name of science is being questioned. Karl Popper and John Eccles, in the preface to their book *The Self and the Brain*, state that:

An additional motive for writing this book is that we both feel that the debunking of man has gone far enough – even too far. It is said that we had to learn from Copernicus and Darwin that man's place in the universe is not so exalted or so exclusive as once thought. That may well be. But since Copernicus we have learned to appreciate how wonderful and rare, perhaps even unique, our little Earth is in this big universe, and since Darwin we have learned more about the incredible organization of all living things on Earth, and also about the unique position of man among his fellow creatures.[188]

Popper and Eccles present arguments in favour of a 'dualist' model of the mind that preserves its self-identity, uniqueness and autonomy. They emphasize the interaction of mind and body, where physical and mental states have a separate but interdependent existence. Although not in agreement with all traditional views of the mind, the spirit of their philosophy is much more in line with pre-modern approaches than modern ones. Popper and Eccles also present much evidence to show that the concept of mind and body being separate but interacting entities is a very old belief. 'Dualism', they write, 'is as old as any historical or archaeological evidence reaches . . . All thinkers of whom we know enough to say anything definite on their position, up to and including Descartes, were dualist interactionists.'[189] Their work supports the observation that at all times throughout history, in all parts of the world, human experience has led to the belief that the mind is immaterial, and somehow independent of the body.

Geoffrey Madell, in his book *Mind and Materialism*, also presents arguments in favour of 'dualism', arguing that the mind is autonomous and functions by the interaction of its material and immaterial parts. To what extent these arguments opposing to the mainstream reductionist approach to the human mind will reverse the uncritical acceptance of empiricism in the modern view of science remains to be seen.

One important point to bear in mind about discussions on the existence of an immortal soul in humans is that the terms of the discussion must remain firmly in the realm of our experience. This is the 'positive' contribution of the philosophy of positivism. A soul can only be understood in terms of its effects, and it is not possible to discuss the nature of the soul without reference to human beings and their qualities. One cannot, for instance, meaningfully understand the nature of the souls of 'angels', or 'spirits'. One cannot, as was previously attempted, understand a hierarchy of souls stretching beyond humanity. For the spiritual nature of human beings or the concept of God to have any meaning, they must first be related to something within our experience.

The above discussion only touches upon some of the many complex issues involved in trying to describe the mind in empirical and physical terms. Much has been written on this subject, but despite the many difficulties involved in describing the mind in such terms, most modern philosophies take this approach. Their common weakness lies in estimating just how fundamental the problems of the mind are. The mysteries surrounding the nature of the mind cannot be solved by methods that depend on the mystery itself. On cannot, for instance, solve the problem of where the laws of physics come from by using the laws of physics; similarly, every attempt at solving fundamental problems of the mind will use the very qualities that are under examination.

Our modern external approach to discovering the truth, as already discussed, not only hinders us from understanding human nature, but also prevents us from understanding the concept of God. For Descartes, and in all the world's spiritual traditions, God forms an indubitable part of human character. Descartes found God to be an inner discovery, an indwelling spiritual experience that could not be approached in external terms. A common misinterpretation of Descartes' theories is that he proved God's existence from the very idea of God in his mind. But this only illustrates the modern bias towards approaching the concept of God in external terms, placing primary importance on external verification. Descartes was never in doubt that his belief in God was pre-empirical, pre-rational, and a spiritual instinct. Descartes' conclusion that God formed the primary ground of all human knowledge, and modern adverse reactions to this conclusion, help to illustrate that the traditional approach to God in terms of an indwelling spiritual experience has been largely changed into one that approaches the concept of God in external terms, separate from human nature. In the past, the concept of God was inseparable from the very best, the most distinctive, the most noble part of human nature.

The central role of God in Descartes' philosophy, providing a crucial link between the inner universe of the mind and the external universe, serves to emphasize the modern dilemma of a disembodied, subjective self separated from the body of an empirically dominated, impersonal universe. In Descartes' philosophy, the unity of mind and body is mediated by God; it is a tripartite system, not a dualistic one, as it is often considered to be.

The unity of mind and body depends on our experience of God, yet the vitality of this spiritual experience has been progressively lost over the past few centuries. The western mind has become more and more secularized in the face of ever-worsening religious conflicts and divisions. In a spiritually fragmented world, what can unite body and mind? All attempts at describing either the mind wholly in terms of the body, or the body in terms of the mind, ignore their obvious fundamental differences.

Modern attempts to understand human nature are of course valuable. There are certainly animal-like and robot-like characteristics in human nature. But is that all there is? The dogmatic attempt to deny other elements in human nature, and even to invoke the authority of science to support such a claim, is the attitude challenged by this book.

The more science progresses, the deeper the mysteries of the universe and the mind appear to be. The discoveries of science do not take away the mysteries of the universe, they deepen them. The claim that science eliminates mystery from our world is characteristic of the spiritual confusion that dominates our modern age. It is essentially closed-minded, and imposes distinct conceptual boundaries on our understanding of the universe, where in reality there are none.

If history teaches anything, it teaches us that our understanding of the universe is open-ended. There is a natural logic to being open-minded, and a fundamental self-defeat in every attempt to place limitations on our description of human nature. The scientific spirit lies much more in affirming the presence of universal mysteries, than in rejecting them in favour of techniques and impersonal observations.

It is now generally recognized that we are living in a time of ecological crisis. Our modern life in cities has numbed our sensitivity to nature; the concrete environment in which most of us grow up is making the natural world more and more remote from our experience, and we are only now beginning to understand what is being lost. Our experience of life as a whole is dominated by artificiality, and this loss of 'natural' experience dulls our appreciation of the cosmological questions about life. Like the receding countryside, issues such as the nature and existence of

God, the meaning of life, and the existence of a moral order are being marginalized. The modern mind tends to seek seclusion behind empiricist and secular walls, content to engage only with the more superficial layers of human existence.

But if the spiritual instinct does not find release in the normal channels, it will find others. With the decline of orthodox religion, many cults have arisen to fill the spiritual vacuum, and ideologies such as militant communism and nationalism have taken on the character of religious faith.

Human minds have the capacity to move through an open universe. There has been no single discovery or set of discoveries that has undermined the evidence of our freedom and uniqueness – indeed the success of modern science is founded upon human uniqueness and autonomy; over the past 400 years, the gulf that separates human beings from all other forms of life on this planet has widened dramatically. Our mental evolution has eclipsed all forms of biological evolution.

The lessons that the Copernican revolution can teach us about the inner universe have been misunderstood. A Copernican revolution in our moral universe does not leave it without a centre, but involves us in discovering a new spiritual sun – a centre around which all the significant elements of our experience revolve.

It is my hope that the preceding pages may contribute something towards restating the importance of the universal mysteries underlying our experience of being human, and in particular, towards reinforcing belief in the spiritual nature of the mind: that it is immaterial, autonomous, creative, unique, and the means by which we make an inner journey to fulfil a life-purpose. I also hope this book can contribute to a renewed openness in learning from the world's collective store of traditional wisdom, and to appreciating the great universal mysteries that underlie science. In our modern age, these things are all too easily lost to our sight.

But there is something more. If we are actors in a cosmic drama, then the theatre is within each of us. The inner drama is animated by the different selves of human nature. All members of the cast have their respective parts to play, but it is only when the moral self takes centre stage that our lives take on meaning or can be of benefit to anyone else. Only the moral self has the capacity to seek out truth and set us on the journey of self-discovery. Recently, however, we have been encouraged to take an off-stage role, the role of a spectator, but we must resist this. Our destiny, our fate, lies in being on centre stage. We must endeavour to uncover our eyes and ears, open our hearts and minds, so that we can recognize our role, play our part, and discover just who we really are.

Notes

••

1. W. Shakespeare, *Hamlet*, II, ii

2. I. Kant, *Kant Selections: Critique of Practical Reason*, ed. L. W. Breck, p. 325

3. F. W. Matson, *The Broken Image*, p. v–vi

4. A. N. Whitehead, *The Concept of Nature*, p. 26–48

5. C. P. Snow, *The Two Cultures: A Second Look*

6. J. Macmurray, *Freedom in the Modern World*, p. 29

7. G. Ryle, *The Concept of Mind*, p. 17

8. B. Russell, 'A Free Man's Worship' in *Mysticism and Logic*

9. K. R. Popper and J. C. Eccles, *The Self and Its Brain*, p. 3

10. A. D. Lindsay, *Religion, Science and Society in the Modern World*, p. 40

11. P. Sherrad, *The Rape of Man and Nature*, Chapter 4

12. R. Sheldrake, *The Rebirth of Nature*, Chapters 1 and 2

13. T. Roszak, *Where the Wasteland Ends*, p. 156

14. P. Sherrad, *The Rape of Man and Nature*, p. 88

15. P. Tillich, *Theology of Culture*. Man 'has become a part of the reality he has created, an object among objects, a thing among things, a cog within a universal machine to which he must adapt himself in order not to be smashed by it' (p. 46).

16. P. Sherrad, *The Rape of Man and Nature*, p. 79

17. P. Tillich, quoted by F. Matson, *The Broken Image*, p. iii

18. A. J. Toynbee, *An Historian's Approach to Religion*, p. 146

19. J. Durant, ed., *Darwinism and Divinity*, p. 9

20. J. Marks, *Science and the Making of the Modern World*, p. 36

21. B. Russell, *History of Western Philosophy*, p. 512

22. B. Russell, *Religion and Science*, p. 19

23. Ibid., pp. 24–5

24. A. Koestler, *The Sleepwalkers*, p. 220

25. Alfred, Lord Tennyson, 'In Memoriam 3'

26. J. Marks, *Science and the Making of the Modern World*, pp. 32–43

27. A. Koestler, *The Sleepwalkers*, pp. 431–503

28. Ibid., p. 264

29. Attributed to Hussayn Ali, in *The Writings of Bahá'u'lláh*, p. 40

30. F. Matson, *The Broken Image*, Chapter 1

31. Ibid., p. vi

32. E. A. Burtt, *The Metaphysical Foundations of Science*, pp. 238–9

33. Ibid., p. 88

34. Ibid.

35. A. N. Whitehead, *Science and the Modern World*, p. 70

36. F. Capra, *The Turning Point*, p. 45

37. W. Barret, *Death of the Soul*, p. 20

38. G. Ryle, *The Concept of Mind*, p. 17

39. E. Anscombe and P. T. Geach, eds., *Descartes: Philosophical Writings*, p. xxxv

40. F. Capra, *The Turning Point*, p. 44

41. T. Roszak, *Where the Wasteland Ends*, p. 253

42. Ibid., p. 264

43. F. Matson, *The Broken Image*, p. 6

44. J. R. Vrooman, *Rene Descartes*, p. 189

45. E. Anscombe and P. T. Geach, eds., *Descartes: Philosophical Writings*, p. 26

46. R. Sheldrake, *The Rebirth of Nature*, p. 32

47. Ibid., p. 32

48. T. Roszak, *Where the Wasteland Ends*, pp. 163–74

49. J. Spedding, R. L. Ellis and D. D. Heath, eds., *The Works of Francis Bacon*, Vol. IV, p. 20

50. D. Hume, *A Treatise of Human Nature*, p. 60

51. Ibid., p. 300

52. Ibid., p. 301

53. B. Russell, *Why I Am Not a Christian*, p. 140

54. B. Russell, *History of Western Philosophy*, p. 788

55. D. Hume, *An Enquiry Concerning Human Understanding and Concerning the Principles of Morals*, sec. 7.3

56. D. Hume, *A Treatise of Human Nature*, p. 463

57. D. Hume, *Dialogues Concerning Natural Religion*, introduction

58. D. Hume, *A Treatise of Human Nature*, pp. 267–8

59. F. Matson, *The Broken Image*, p. 18

60. Ibid.

61. W. T. Stace, *Religion and the Modern World*, p. 173

62. F. Matson, *The Broken Image*, pp. 34–6

63. E. Nagel and J. R. Newman, *Godel's Proof*, Chapters 4 and 5

64. Ibid., pp. 8–25

65. R. Carnap, 'The Old and New Logic', in A. J. Ayer, ed., *Logical Positivism*, p. 133

66. Ibid., p. 145

67. Ibid.

68. Put to me during a live radio interview for BBC Radio Oxford, Oxford, 1988

69. A. J. Ayer, *Language, Truth and Logic*, pp. 9–10

70. Ibid., p. 106

71. Ibid., p. 110

72. Ibid., p. 16

73. E. Nagel and J. R. Newman, *Godel's Proof*, Chapters 7 and 8

74. B. Magee, *Modern British Philosophy*, p. 77

75. Ibid., p. 87

76. Ibid., pp. 20–1

77. F. Matson, *The Broken Image*, p. 30

78. Ibid., p. 62

79. T. Roszak, *Where the Wasteland Ends*, pp. 167–8

80. F. Matson, *The Broken Image*, p. 47

81. A. Maslow, *The Psychology of Science*, p. 42

82. T. Paine, *The Rights of Man*, p. 110

83. A. N. Whitehead, *Science and the Modern World*, pp. 94–5

84. J. Searle, *Minds, Brains, and Science, The 1984 Reith Lectures*, p. 30

85. Ibid., p. 30

86. D. Hofstadter and D. C. Dennett, *The Mind's I*, pp. 53–5

87. P. N. Johnson-Laird, *The Computer and the Mind*

88. I. Aleksander and H. Morton, *An Introduction to Neural Computing*

89. For a detailed discussion on how such computers are unable to account for human intentionality and human interpretations, see G. Madell, *Mind and Materialism*.

90. See R. Penrose, *The Emperor's New Mind*, for a detailed discussion on the inherent limits of computer algorithms in describing mathematics.

91. M. Midgley, 'The Religion of Evolution' in J. Durant, ed., *Darwinism and Divinity: Essays on Evolution and Religious Belief*

92. Hans Kung, *Does God Exist?*, p. 207

93. Ibid., p. 192

94. M. Midgley, in *Darwinism and Divinity*, p. 156

95. J. Monod, *Chance and Necessity*, p. 110

96. R. Dawkins, *The Blind Watchmaker*, p. ix–x

97. C. Darwin, *The Origin of Species*, p. 115

98. K. Lorenz, *On Human Aggression*

99. D. Morris, *The Naked Ape*

100. D. Morris, *The Human Zoo*

101. K. Lorenz, *On Human Aggression*, concluding paragraph

102. Ibid.

103. M. Midgley, *Evolution as a Religion*, pp. 140–1

104. Quoted by R. Trigg, *Ideas of Human Nature*, pp. 87–8

105. J. D. Barrow and F. J. Tipler, *The Anthropic Cosmological Principle*

106. E. Fromm, *The Anatomy of Human Destructiveness*, p. 148

107. Ibid., p. 576

108. Ibid., pp. 284–5

109. *Medicine and War* (journal), Vol. 3, 1987, pp. 191–3

110. K. Popper, *Logic of Scientific Discovery*, pp. 40–2. For a discussion on the limits of falsifiability as a methodology in science, see A. F. Chalmers, *What is This Thing Called Science?*, and D. Stanesby, *Science, Reason and Religion*, pp. 69–73.

111. T. S. Kuhn, *The Structure of Scientific Revolutions*

112. A. F. Chalmers, *What is This Thing Called Science?*

113. Ibid., Chapters 4, 5, 6, 8, and 12

114. M. Polanyi, *Science, Faith and Society*

115. I. Kant, *Critique of Pure Reason*, p. 183

116. D. Hume, *A Treatise of Human Nature*, p. 123

117. Ibid., p. 125

118. D. Hume, *A Treatise of Human Nature*, p. 153

119. M. Polanyi, *Personal Knowledge*, p. 272

120. M. Polanyi and H. Prosch, *Meaning*, pp. 40–1

121. Ibid., pp. 61–2

122. F. Nietzsche, *Will to Power*

123. A. Einstein, *Out of My Later Years*, p. 26

124. M. Polanyi and H. Prosch, *Meaning*, p. 56

125. Ibid., p. 63

126. E. Fromm, *Man For Himself*, p. 105

127. M. Polanyi, *A Study of Man*, p. 96

128. M. Polanyi and H. Prosch, *Meaning*, p. 181

129. H. M. Balyuzi, *'Abdu'l-Bahá*, p. 73

130. W. James, *The Will to Believe: Human Immortality*, p. 93

131. F. E. Manuel, *A Portrait of Isaac Newton*, pp. 388–9

132. See for example F. E. Manuel, *A Portrait of Isaac Newton*, Chapter 15

133. A. Einstein, *Out of My Later Years*, p. 61

134. G. Holton and Y. Elkana, *Albert Einstein*, p. 242

135. A. Einstein, *Out of My Later Years*, p. 29

136. A. Pais, *Subtle is the Lord: The Science and Life of Albert Einstein*

137. Ibid., p. 178

138. G. Holton and Y. Elkana, *Albert Einstein*, p. 225

139. Ibid., pp. 225–6

140. A. Einstein, 'Autobiographical Notes' in Paul A. Schilpp, ed., *Albert Einstein: Philosopher-Scientist*

141. M. Polanyi in *Personal Knowledge*, pp. 9–13, suggests that the Michelson–Morely experiment was far from conclusive, and that Einstein founded his postulate on a demand that Maxwell's equations be invariant. An example of a typical textbook that wrongly stresses the importance of the Michelson–Morely experiment in the history of special relativity is *Fundamentals of Modern Physics*, by R. E. Eisberg, pp. 9–16

142. A. Einstein, *Ideas and Opinions*, p. 24

143. Ibid., p. 23

144. Ibid., p. 22

145. W. Heisenberg, *Physics and Beyond*

146. Ibid., pp. 208–10

147. R. Weber, *Dialogues with Scientists and Sages*, p. 8

148. B. Russell, *History of Western Philosophy*, p. 512

149. D. B. Barrett, ed., *World Christian Encyclopedia*. The statistics are: 91.2% religious people in the United Kingdom (86.9% Christian), 93.3% religious people in America (88% Christian), and 96.3% religious people in Germany (92.8% Christian).

150. J. Sacks, *The Persistence of Faith: The 1990 Reith Lectures*, p. 3

151. W. T. Jones, *The Sciences and the Humanities*, p. 17

152. Quoted by F. Matson, *The Broken Image*, p. 66

153. A. Einstein, *Ideas and Opinions*, p. 45

154. O. Nathan and H. Norden, *Einstein on Peace*

155. Ibid., pp. 440–9

156. Ibid., pp. xii

157. Ibid., p. 388

158. Ibid., pp. 555–6

159. Ibid., p. 161

160. A. Einstein, *Ideas and Opinions*, p. 44

161. E. Laszlo et al., *Goals for Mankind: A Report to the Club of Rome on the New Horizons of Global Community*

162. E. Laszlo, *The Inner Limits of Mankind*, pp. 25–6

163. Ibid., p. 32

164. Ibid., p. 34

165. B. Russell, *History of Western Philosophy*, pp. 481–2

166. *The Book of Common Prayer*, p. 336

167. J. Marks, *Science and the Making of the Modern World*, p. 91

168. A. Maslow, *The Psychology of Science*, p. 33

169. E. Fromm, *To Have or To Be*, pp. 49–50

170. Bahá'u'lláh, *Gleanings from the Writings of Bahá'u'lláh*, pp. 51–2

171. K. R. Popper, *A Pocket Popper*, ed. D. Miller, pp. 127–8

172. K. R. Popper, *The Open Universe*, p. 130

173. K. R. Popper, *Unended Quest: An Intellectual Autobiography*, p. 80

174. Bahá'u'lláh, *Gleanings from the Writings of Bahá'u'lláh*, p. 65

175. Ibid., p. 73. The founder of the Bahá'í Faith, Bahá'u'lláh, refers to the founders of religions as 'Primary Mirrors of the Divine Being'. On p. 114 of *Some Answered Questions*, by 'Abdu'l-Bahá, son of Bahá'u'lláh, the founders of religion are described as being 'a clear mirror in which the Sun of Reality becomes visible and manifest with all its qualities and perfections'.

176. R. Swinburne, *The Existence of God*. Surveys the arguments for and against the existence of God, and discusses a balance of probability: theism is probable only in relation to the improbability of any rival view. On p. 290 he writes: 'Theism is perhaps very unlikely, but it is far more likely than any rival supposition.'

177. B. Russell, *Why I Am Not a Christian*, pp. 133–53

178. P. Davies, *The Mind of God*. See p. 70, where modern cosmological theories about a universe are referred to in terms of a 'mother sheet' giving birth to a 'Child'.

179. Bahá'u'lláh, *The Kitáb-I-Iqán*. See pp. 71–5, where the corruption of religion is likened to clouds blocking out the

original teachings and spirit of a religion. In these pages,
Bahá'u'lláh interprets the New Testament prophecy of the
'Son of Man coming in the clouds of heaven'. He states that
this prophecy is to be correctly understood in terms of Christ
returning at a time when the light of religious faith is obscured.

180. K. Cambell, *Body and Mind.* See pp. 57–8: 'The bulk of recent
thought on the Mind-Body problem has involved denying
the dual character of man. As the materiality of the body
enjoys massive scientific support, the spirituality of the mind
has been the favourite casualty.'

181. S. Weinberg, *First Three Minutes*

182. 'Abdu'l-Bahá gives the seed/tree analogy on p. 205 of *Some
Answered Questions* and on pp. 96–99 of *Paris Talks*. Also in
Some Answered Questions, p. 240, the human soul is said to
have a specific identity from its beginning.

183. 'Abdu'l-Bahá, *Some Answered Questions*, p. 228

184. Ibid., p. 239

185. J. Hatcher, *The Purpose of Physical Reality*, p. 151

186. Bahá'u'lláh, *Gleanings from the Writings of Bahá'u'lláh*, pp. 156–7.
See also pp. 47–8, 'Abdu'l-Bahá, *Promulgation of Universal Peace.*

187. A. Toynbee, *Change and Habit*, p. 14

188. K. Popper and J. Eccles, *The Self and Its Brain*, p. vii

189. Ibid., p. 152

Bibliography

'Abdu'l-Bahá. *Promulgation of Universal Peace*, Illinois, Bahá'í
    Publishing Trust, 1978
— *Paris Talks*, London, Bahá'í Publishing Trust, 1979
— *Some Answered Questions*, Illinois, Bahá'í Publishing Trust, 1984
Aleksander, I. and Morton, H. *An Introduction to Neural
    Computing*, London, Chapman and Hall, 1990
Anscombe, E. and Geach, P. T., eds., *Descartes: Philosophical
    Writings*, London, Nelson's University Paperbacks, 1954
Ayer, A. J., ed., *Logical Positivism*, New York, The Free Press, 1959
— *Language, Truth and Logic*, Middlesex, Penguin Books, 1971
Bahá'u'lláh. *The Kitáb-I-Iqán*, Illinois, Bahá'í Publishing Trust,
    1950
— *Gleanings from the Writings of Bahá'u'lláh*, London, Bahá'í
    Publishing Trust, 1978
— *The Writings of Bahá'u'lláh*, New Delhi, Bahá'í Publishing
    Trust, 1986
Balyuzi, H. M. *'Abdu'l-Bahá*, Oxford, George Ronald, 1972
Barret, W. *Death of the Soul*, Oxford, Oxford University Press, 1987
Barrett, D. B., ed., *World Christian Encyclopedia*, Oxford, Oxford
    University Press, 1982
Barrow, J. D. and Tipler, F. J. *The Anthropic Cosmological Principle*,
    Oxford, Clarendon Press, 1986
Burtt, E. A. *The Metaphysical Foundations of Science*, London,
    Routledge and Kegan Paul, 1949
Cambell, K. *Body and Mind*, Indiana, University of Notre Dame
    Press, 1984
Capra, F. *The Turning Point*, London, Fontana Books, 1983

Chalmers, A. F. *What is This Thing Called Science?*, Milton Keynes, Open University, 1982

Darwin, C. *The Origin of Species*, Middlesex, Penguin Books, 1968

Davies, P. *The Mind of God*, Middlesex, Penguin Books, 1993

Dawkins, R. *The Blind Watchmaker*, Essex, Longman Scientific and Technical, 1986

Durant, J. ed., *Darwinism and Divinity: Essays on Evolution and Religious Belief*, Oxford, Basil Blackwell, 1986

Einstein, A. *Out of My Later Years*, New Jersey, The Citadel Press, 1956

— *Ideas and Opinions*, London, Souvenir Press, 1973

Eisberg, R. E. *Fundamentals of Modern Physics*, London, John Wiley and Sons, 1961

Fromm, E. *The Anatomy of Human Destructiveness*, Middlesex, Penguin Books, 1977

— *Man For Himself*, London, Routledge and Kegan Paul, 1978

— *To Have or To Be*, London, Abacus Sphere Books, 1979

Hatcher, J. *The Purpose of Physical Reality*, Illinois, Bahá'í Publishing Trust, 1987

Heisenberg, W. *Physics and Beyond*, London, George Allen and Unwin, 1971

Hofstadter, D. and Dennett, D. C. *The Mind's I*, Middlesex, Penguin Books, 1982

Holton, G. and Elkana, Y. *Albert Einstein*, New Jersey, Princeton University Press, 1982

Hume, D. An *Enquiry Concerning Human Understanding and Concerning the Principles of Morals*, Oxford, Clarendon Press, 1975

— *A Treatise of Human Nature*, Middlesex, Penguin Classics, 1984

— *Dialogues Concerning Natural Religion*, Middlesex, Penguin Classics, 1990

James, W. *The Will to Believe: Human Immortality*, New York, Dover Publications, 1956

Johnson-Laird, P. N. *The Computer and the Mind*, London, Fontana Press, 1988

Jones, W. T. *The Sciences and the Humanities*, Berkeley, University of California Press, 1965

Kant, I. *Critique of Pure Reason*, trans. Norman K. Smith, New

York, St Martin's Press, 1929
— *Kant Selections: Critique of Practical Reason*, ed. L. W. Breck, New York, Macmillan, 1988
Koestler, A. *The Sleepwalkers*, Middlesex, Pelican Books, 1968
Kuhn, T. S. *The Structure of Scientific Revolutions*, Chicago, The University of Chicago Press, 1970
Kung, H. *Does God Exist?*, London, Collins Fount Paperbacks, 1980
Laszlo, E. *The Inner Limits of Mankind*, Oxford, Oneworld, 1989
Laszlo, E. et al. *Goals for Mankind: A Report to the Club of Rome on the New Horizons of Global Community*, New York, Dutton, 1977
Lindsay, A. D. *Religion, Science and Society in the Modern World*, Oxford, Oxford University Press, 1943
Lorenz, K. *On Human Aggression*, London, Methuen, 1969
Macmurray, J. *Freedom in the Modern World*, London, Faber and Faber, 2nd edn., 1935
Madell, G. *Mind and Materialism*, Edinburgh, Edinburgh University Press, 1988
Magee, B. *Modern British Philosophy*, Oxford, Oxford University Press, 1986
Manuel, F. E. *A Portrait of Isaac Newton*, New York, Da Capo Press, 1968
Marks, J. *Science and the Making of the Modern World*, London, Heinemann, 1983
Maslow, A. *The Psychology of Science*, New York, Harper and Row, 1966
Matson, F. W. *The Broken Image*, New York, Anchor Books, 1966
Midgley, M. *Evolution as a Religion*, London, Methuen and Co., 1985
Miller, D., ed., *A Pocket Popper*, London, Fontana Press, 1983
Monod, J. *Chance and Necessity*, London, Collins, 1972
Morris, D. *The Naked Ape*, London, Jonathan Cape, 1967
— *The Human Zoo*, New York, Dell, 1981
Nagel, E. and Newman, J. R. *Godel's Proof*, New York, New York University Press, 1958
Nathan, O. and Norden, H. *Einstein on Peace*, London, Methuen and Co., 1963

Nietzsche, F. *Will to Power*, trans. W. Kaufmann and R. J. Hollingdale, New York, Random House, 1968

Paine, T. *The Rights of Man*, New York, Penguin Classics, 1985

Pais, A. *Subtle is the Lord: The Science and Life of Albert Einstein*, Oxford, Oxford University Press, 1983

Penrose, R. *The Emperor's New Mind*, Oxford, Oxford University Press, 1989

Polanyi, M. *Science, Faith and Society*, Oxford, Oxford University Press, 1946

— *Personal Knowledge*, London, Routledge and Kegan Paul, 1958

— *A Study of Man*, London, Routledge and Kegan Paul, 1958

Polanyi, M. and Prosch, H. *Meaning*, Chicago, University of Chicago Press, 1975

Popper, K. R. *The Open Universe*, London, Hutchinson, 1982

— *Unended Quest, An Intellectual Autobiography*, London, Fontana Paperbacks, 1986

— *Logic of Scientific Discovery*, London, Unwin Hyman, 1990.

Popper, K. R. and Eccles, J. C. *The Self and Its Brain*, London, Routledge and Kegan Paul, 1983

Roszak, T. *Where the Wasteland Ends*, California, Celestial Arts, 1989

Russell, B. *Mysticism and Logic and Other Essays*, London, Allen and Unwin, 1917

— *Religion and Science*, Oxford, Oxford University Press, 1961

— *Why I Am Not a Christian*, London, Unwin Paperbacks, 1975

— *History of Western Philosophy*, London, Counterpoint, 1984

Ryle, G. *The Concept of Mind*, Middlesex, Penguin Books, 1963

Sacks, J. *The Persistence of Faith: The 1990 Reith Lectures*, London, Weidenfeld and Nicholson, 1991

Schilpp, P. A., ed., *Albert Einstein: Philosopher-Scientist*, Illinois, Open Court, 1970

Searle, J. *Minds, Brains, and Science: The 1984 Reith Lectures*, London, BBC, 1984

Shakespeare, W. *Hamlet*, II, ii

Sheldrake, R. *The Rebirth of Nature*, London, Century, 1990

Sherrad, P. *The Rape of Man and Nature*, Cambridge, Golgonooza Press, 1987

Snow, C. P. *The Two Cultures: A Second Look*, Cambridge,

Cambridge University Press, 1969

Spedding, J., Ellis, R. L. and Heath, D. D., eds., *The Works of Francis Bacon*, London, Longmans, 1870

Stace, W. T. *Religion and the Modern World*, London, Macmillan, 1953

Stanesby, D. *Science, Reason and Religion*, London, Routledge, 1988

Swinburne, R. *The Existence of God*, Oxford, Clarendon Press, 1979

Tennyson, Lord A. 'In Memoriam 3' in *Tennyson's Poetry*, ed. Hill, R. W. Jr., New York, W. W. Norton & Co., 1971

Tillich, P. *Theology of Culture*, Oxford, Oxford University Press, 1964

Toynbee, A. J. *An Historian's Approach to Religion*, Oxford, Oxford University Press, 1956

— *Change and Habit*, Oxford, Oneworld, 1992

Trigg, R. *Ideas of Human Nature*, Oxford, Basil Blackwell, 1988

Vrooman, J. R. *Rene Descartes*, New York, Putnam, 1970

Weber, W. *Dialogues with Scientists and Sages*, London, Arkana, 1990

Weinberg, S. *First Three Minutes*, London, André Deutsch, 1977

Whitehead, A. N. *The Concept of Nature*, Cambridge, Cambridge University Press, 1964

— *Science and the Modern World*, London, Free Association Press Books, 1985

Index